Epic Failures in DevSecOps

VOLUME 2

ISBN: 9798600197497
Imprint: DevSecOps Days Press

Publisher:
DevSecOps Days Press
48 Wall Street, 5th Floor
New York, NY 10005

Editor in Chief: Mark Miller
Copy Editors: Alexis Del Duke, Nikki Mejer, and Melissa Schmidt
Design and Formatting: Melissa Schmidt

www.devsecopsdays.com

Epic Failures in DevSecOps

DevSecOps

VOLUME 2

Eliza May Austin

Marc Cluet

Jaclyn Damiano

Rob England

Jasmine James

Sladjana Jovanovic

Ryan Lockard

Larry Maccherone

Bill McArthur

Chris Riley

Dr. Cherry Vu

Mark Miller, Editor

Contents

Introduction

by Mark Miller

JANUARY 2020

Introduction

Another year, another nine failures. That's just the way it goes when you ask to hear stories about Epic Failures. Everybody's got one.

Last year, in 2019, when we published the first Epic Failures book, we had no idea whether anyone would be interested. Thousands of downloads later, with literally thousands of printed books being handed out at conferences, we now know the truth: The community loves failure. At least hearing about other people's failures.

Volume 2 builds on the momentum created by Volume 1. The quality of this set of stories is outstanding, starting with **"Question Everything"** by the DevSecOps Contrarian herself, Eliza May Austin. Larry Maccherone, **"Shift Left, Not S#!T Left,"** runs through a list of six ways to fail on a project, while **"Making Everyone Visible In Tech"** by Jaclyn Damiano tells a personal story of life transformation through tech. Sladjana Jovanovic and Bill McArthur from TD Bank take on the Herculean task of breaking down silos to create a collaborative environment in **"From Silos to Communities." "What Not to Do When Rolling Out DevSecOps and Other Learnings"** comes from Jasmine James in her work as an IT Manager at Delta Airlines. Marc Cluet takes on cultural transformation in **"Cultural Approaches to Transformations: Staying Safe and Healthy,"** while Ryan Lockard focuses on **"The Seven Deadly Sins of DevSecOps."** Chris Riley asks us the meme-inducing question, **"Did You Try Turning it Off and On?"** when examining simple bugs that have debilitating outcomes, and we finish with IT sceptic Rob England and Dr. Cherry Vu encouraging us to **"Kill the Restructure."**

One of the motivations for publishing a book like this is for you, the reader, to be able to identify with the stories. It is our hope that you will see yourself somewhere within these pages and know you did not screw things up on your own, that you are not unique when it comes to hosing a project, and sometimes you can sit back and laugh after it's all over. It's important to be able to step back and get perspective when something goes wrong — and even better — to let others know what happened.

I'm proud to give these authors the chance to tell their stories and hope it encourages you to let others know about your Epic Failures. Who knows? You might end up telling your story in Volume 3 of Epic Failures in DevSecOps.

Best wishes on your next productive failure.

Mark Miller
Founder and Editor, Epic Failures in DevSecOps
Co-founder, All Day DevOps
Senior Storyteller, Sonatype

CHAPTER 1

Question Everything

by Eliza May Austin

CHAPTER 1

Question Everything

The biggest challenge with making changes is making those changes stick. I think that's only one half of the problem. As a security professional, I'm concerned that some things "stick" too well, becoming unchallengeable, infallible, and immovable. They become the new paradigm and anyone who doesn't "get it" is a heretic. That's how it was for DevOps ten years ago, and it appears to be the case for DevSecOps today. Don't get me wrong, I believe passionately in security and I can see the advantages of a DevSecOps approach. It's just that what I see organisations do on the ground does not always line up with what I believe DevSecOps should be.

In the early days of DevOps there was a saying: "I wouldn't want my life support system developed by DevOps." That made sense. You can't "fail fast and roll back" a person who died because of bugs in the software. This lesson has much to teach us in DevSecOps too. There are times when DevSecOps is the right thing to do. There are times when, despite the name, DevSecOps has delivered some horribly insecure code. We need to get to grips with this before someone outside of Development, Security, or Operations loses faith in us.

Some of you will come from environments where DevSecOps is working perfectly — you have been indoctrinated by the religion, drank the Kool Aid, and see little room left for improvement. I'd ask you to reflect a little. What are you bringing to the table? Is it Dev, Sec, or Ops? I would bet my favourite pair of heels that you're not a security professional. Despite what the name will lead you to believe, DevSecOps is little more than DevOps if you're doing it well. It is, more often than not, nothing more than just another label.

Part of being a security professional involves asking the difficult questions and challenging the status quo, the trends, processes, and hierarchy. The aim of the security professional is to see the wider picture, not concentrate solely on oneself. Overall, the mindset should be: "How can we support the business in XYZ without compromising the security and the integrity of the project or topic in hand?" I'm willing to put myself in the firing line, voice my observations, and hopefully carve out room for improvement. I believe in a future for DevSecOps, but that means I'm willing to take the time to rip it up with the aim of improving it. I see the biggest epic failure of DevSecOps is its ability to help security, and this will be my running theme.

So I ask you, "Is this all hype?" Is this just today's buzzword, trend, or paradigm? What does successful DevSecOps look like? And is it too early to measure success?"

What is DevSecOps Supposed to Achieve?

For all too long developers were pushed to the extremes — technological advances meant more and more developers were required to work harder, longer, and ultimately faster. Pushing out a product that was functional became the measure of success, and for a while this seemed like the way the industry was going. It took security researchers — professional and otherwise — to tap on the window of the corporate world and point out what we now consider to be the low hanging fruit of vulnerabilities before any investment — be that time, financial, or other — was allocated to security.

Fast forward a few more years and security professionals became more than just the geeks who look after the firewall. Security teams became the norm in the big corporates. Infrastructure was secured, architecture improved, and ultimately code was scrutinised. All too often the vulnerabilities found could be fixed with a minor change to the source code — source code that security professionals, quite rightly, have no authority to edit. This led security professionals to "educate" developers on how to rectify the code. The challenge was that these security "fixes" were seen as an afterthought and the same issues would arise again and again. The security professionals became increasingly frustrated and poked at the developers. Despite needing one another and being unable to fulfill the other's role, a friction-driven divide drenched in insecurities and intellectual masturbation ensued. In much the same way Ops "muscled in" on Dev when code became increasingly unsupportable, Sec began to engage more closely with DevOps.

DevSecOps is, in my mind, an unnatural, somewhat forced, but very much needed evolution of a faster and more dynamic digital world. We need to utilise the knowledge of security professionals in the development lifecycle to make applications and systems more secure. We need to bring in the knowledge of IT Ops to make products useful and distributional. Fractured communication channels need repair. They need strengthening and DevSecOps needs to become a *thing* — and to some degree it has — but simply using the terminology doesn't mean the process is actually working.

What DevSecOps Has Given Us

Sadly, what we've ended up with is a hollow, weird, almost religious ideological system that is too open to interpretation and equally resistant to debate — a stereotypical paradigm. It's tangible enough that it can warrant a job title and a team, but fluffy enough that by design it lacks process and constraint. For example, some of us understand DevSecOps to be a method by which to enact cultural change, and others of us see it as a way to align a role or department. So we end up with a very vague understanding of what DevSecOps should be. Is it a hyped up new department with DevSecOps engineers? A renamed developer team? Or a fundamental way of working that doesn't seek to merge roles, but rather deconstruct barriers to enable knowledge sharing? The latter, I would argue, is the correct way to define DevSecOps.

If DevSecOps were to be successfully adopted, DevSecOps engineers, teams, and departments wouldn't exist. DevSecOps should be a way of working — a framework that attempts to heal a misaligned array of technology functions in the business setting.

The Problem With Security

Stepping away from Dev and Ops for a moment, let's take a frank, no-holds-barred look at cyber security. Before I start, I wish to make it known that I love cyber security. It spans all industries and is a phenomenally interesting industry to work in. I wouldn't wish to work in another community. However, I strongly believe that to really improve something, it needs to be analysed, questioned, and debated, and has to be open to critique. If it isn't, it simply is too fragile and not fit for purpose and I have more respect for my industry than to believe it's above critique. So, here goes:

Cyber security is pointlessly introspective. We have a number of different departments and roles and each brings a different self-constructed narrative that makes it elusive to the other. To put it bluntly, there's too much ego. Look at penetration testing: it's predicated on talented individuals who do a huge service to not only technology, but to other industries as well. By breaking things, they improve them. The effects of this span medicine, aviation, the arts, manufacturing, and many other fields. However, there's an undercurrent that sets them apart from SOC analysts and Blue Teamers. The banter screams "defence is beneath me," despite the fact that we all work in defence. The Offensive Team often doesn't communicate findings to the Defensive Team and defenders are left to decipher pen-test reports on their own, when simply having a conversation would help them get things done in a quarter of the time. But they aren't alone.

I believe the noise around the skill shortage has created a complacency issue in SOCs, where all too many people lack ingenuity or the ability to understand the attacker's tactics, techniques, and processes and instead rely solely on tools. Blue Teamers often see an ego problem in the offensive security side so they don't bother to engage. On the flip side, Red Teamers see nothing but "ticket monkeys'" when they look at a SOC (and sometimes they are right). Ultimately, two fundamental technical teams that would produce magic if they worked together, instead become completely disengaged with each other. Throw into the mix GRC being labelled as "pencil pushers" who fail to make the distinction between being compliant and being secure, and you have a further disenfranchised security industry. Expecting security to simply jump onboard the "Happy-Happy-DevSecOps-Rainbow-Culture Train" isn't going to just happen without proof that it works, and quite rightly so.

Dysfunctional Relationships in Cyber Security

PLAYING GAMES

Once, at a retail company, we ran Blue and Red Team engagements under gamification. Allow me to explain how this worked. Blues got points for seeing, recording and stopping Red Team activities and Red Teamers got points for finding vulnerabilities and exploiting them, collecting bonus points if they went undetected. The winners were awarded prizes at the end of each month. Sounds simple, right? It wasn't. We had a huge issue with Red Teamers finding vulnerabilities in systems but not telling anyone, so they could cash them in nearer the end of the month and gain more points in one chunk. All the while, the vulnerabilities remained exposed. The one-upmanship of the Red Team subverted the goal of making the company more secure. Ego got in the way.

SCARED SILENT

Here is another example of the lack of respect for security functions within cyber security by their peers in security. An MSSP I worked with/for a large SOC employed with varying skill sets and a separate team carrying the title "security engineering." This team managed the tools that the SOC used and deployed the products that the MSSP sold to their customers. Because the SOC were using these tools along with data from client environments each day, it was up to them to make recommendations for refinement of these tools to the engineering team.

Although it is common sense that this is the way to run the refinement process, all of the junior members of the SOC were too scared to propose refinements to the engineering team. And, the Senior Analysts that suggested refinements were often dismissed by the Security Engineering team. I remember a heated altercation where I was told that, as a Senior Analyst, I had no place telling an engineer how to refine the tools —the very tools I was using every day! That says it all, doesn't it?

Essentially, the talent needed for the Sec in DevSecOps is currently working in a cultural minefield. An easy integration into these foreign lands, where a whole new cultural adaptation is needed, is not going to happen without a little coaxing and a lot of guidance.

SO CLOSE AND YET SO FAR

Speaking of dysfunction, I was at a large corporation for some time, and although they had a DevSecOps team, it resided in another city and the security team had no contact with them. This company also had Ops and Devs in their own teams, but on different continents. What was the point of this?

NOT MY PROBLEM

A company I consulted at via an MSSP pushed out an application on an externally facing platform, and it was DDoSed within minutes. When questioned how the application was sent into the world in such a poor and insecure state, the response was, "well, it went through the DevSecOps team!" This added another layer of animosity between DevSecOps and other teams. The DevSecOps team, by definition, should not be allowing poorly configured systems to enter production, and they certainly should not be seen as an alternative to a security team, especially if there already is a security team. What a way to add in more bureaucracy!

However, many organisations continue to make this same mistake with DevSecOps — a new silo that consists mainly of developers. I'm definitely not knocking developers here — I want to help them, and I don't think it's okay to expect developers to suddenly be experts in security. Security professionals, by and large, aren't developers and developers aren't security professionals, hence the need for DevSecOps. So, why are we expecting extensive requirements of everyone, rather than a shared understanding among many? What these observations taught me is that we are expecting DevSecOps engineers to be experts in multiple, complex disciplines. Where is this magic unicorn? Who is this master of code, genie of operational IT, and a Jedi of security? Each of these disciplines takes mastery in and of themselves. What on earth are we doing calling this a single job role? Who are we trying to kid? A part of me thinks it's a money-saving exercise, getting one person to do the job of three and by calling it something fancy. This is not what DevSecOps is about.

Business Implementation

A study conducted by the managed services provider Claranet states that 88% of UK businesses have adopted DevSecOps, or plan to within the next 2-5 years, yet only 19% are confident about security integration. Here again is the giant pink elephant in the room. Essentially this survey tells us that companies have adopted DevOps but called it DevSecOps, right? When we take into account that, by design, DevOps outpaces security and business processes, this is just going to further feed problems. Are we just knowingly putting business and personal data at an increased risk of compromise, while claiming to be doing the opposite?

Asking the Industry

If you've ever met me at a conference you may be aware that I'll randomly ask, "What do you do?" and "What's your take on DevSecOps?" There's no judgement here, I'm just taking a simple poll. Here's what I've found:

Developers tend to find DevSecOps an exciting prospect — and quite rightly an excellent opportunity to learn more — and this attitude is awesome. Those currently working in environments where DevSecOps has been adopted already see that it works and produces great results, and overall they are having a positive experience.

When I come across people who are DevSecOps Engineers, DevSecOps Analysts, or even DevSecOps Evangelists (WTF is that?), they have a very aggressive, protective stance about DevSecOps, as if merely questioning its fabric is a direct attack on them. This tells me the fabric from which their role is built is a fragile one at best. I'm becoming increasingly concerned at the rate with which people are labelling themselves DevSecOps Experts and how that will impact the movement. Self proclaimed experts make me nervous.

Meetups and conferences that I attend usually are security focused; however, I do make a conscious and deliberate effort to attend Dev / DevSecOps, and general tech events to expose myself to different ideas. I try not to remain in a bubble of self-imposed egotistical solitude.

When I ask security professionals their opinion on DevSecOps, and granted this is who I speak with most often, I am met with responses that appear to match the same distinct narrative: I can't say much about it really, I don't work in DevSecOps," Or, "I don't have much involvement in that department, so I don't know." Essentially DevSecOps is viewed as a completely different department from security. Not good.

That Podcast

I was invited to participate in an All Day DevOps podcast with Mark Miller, and we had a light-hearted discussion about DevSecOps. From this, I was labelled the "DevSecOps Contrarian." I went on making the assumption that everyone knew DevSecOps was failing, but Mark was adamant that I was mistaken; DevSecOps is working and he wanted to prove it to me. We'd both shared a prime example of communication failure from our individual silos. Yet, I knew it wasn't working and he knew that it was. After the podcast however we were met with feedback that further validated my critique. Many people felt relieved that someone finally came out and said it.

A fun, but hugely abridged list of the comments I received were:

> » "Thank fuck you said it!"
>
> » "I was thinking the same thing."
>
> » "Nothing's changed [after adopting DSO] where I work either."
>
> » "Clearly you're dumb."
>
> » "You are misunderstanding DevSecOps."

Why Security Isn't Engaged

It's fair to ask why security is not more engaged with Dev and Ops, given that we all recognise the advantages of working together. It might be helpful to deconstruct some of the challenges that Security professionals face on a daily basis, to better understand why they find it difficult to take on even more responsibility.

BURN-OUT IN SECURITY

Burn-out is a huge issue in cyber security. I don't know many people who have been in the industry longer than five years and have not been completely burnt out by it. My theory on this is that it's because things are constantly evolving. You will never master security because, tomorrow, there will be a new development that you need to learn the security around (whether it's offence or defence is irrelevant). You're never going to feel a sense of satisfaction that you know your craft completely. This is probably why it's well known that rates of imposter syndrome in security are shockingly high.

There isn't a solid way to quantitatively measure the metrics of security success. If a SOC analyst is responding to incidents, how many are enough to consider it a successful day? What we deem as success in security, in its rawest form, is "not being compromised." But how does such a vague end goal end in individual job satisfaction? Has a threat hunter who didn't find anything actually failed? What if they feel like a failure, so they just keep hunting and hunting and hunting and when they were supposed to go home at 6:00 PM they are still there at 1:00 AM sifting through network traffic to try and find something to legitimise themselves? This happens. As for forensics, once I couldn't find evidence of malice to prove or disprove a theory. And although I couldn't find it, I couldn't stop looking because I didn't know if I couldn't find it because I was bad at my job or because it wasn't there. I was determined to prove I wasn't rubbish so I just kept going. That really isn't sustainable.

Security doesn't have a tangible endpoint, where "enough is done now" and "security is complete." With developers, the product is complete when it's functional and deemed to be so. With Ops the project is complete when its rolled out successfully and everyone has signed off on it. Security is complete when... well, never. We never reach a point when security is done.

STIGMA WHEN STRUGGLING

I've witnessed a key challenge in security where people aren't willing to admit when they don't know something. Throw into this situation the ego of some security factions and you have a recipe for a frustrating and uncomfortable work environment. One of the most difficult aspects of the job is actually having to retain so much knowledge. It's increasingly difficult to remain current.

There are over two thousand security tools on the market, and in any one environment you can be expected to know how to use up to 100 of them, maybe a dozen day to day. Simply not knowing is often treated as unacceptable. Personally I believe there are no such things as stupid *questions*. It's stupid *people* who don't question anything. But this isn't the norm; the security industry talks the talk on mental-health awareness, imposter syndrome, and collaboration, but there is still so much stigma attached to admitting you don't know something. In my opinion, this is an obvious reason for the lack of new blood in the sector.

OVERWORKED

There's a systemic cultural problem in service providers. MSSPs, even the big names, are known to over-promise and under-deliver. Sales people, service managers, and C-level hotshots make a career out of overzealous but well intentioned customer engagement. But when the over-promised inundation of work needs to be carried out, fixing the bad practices of the business and the heavy weight of its reputational purity must be borne upon the technologist's shoulders.

DevSecOps is just another thing that hasn't proven itself yet.

I can't speak for everyone in security, (and I don't try to!), but this is certainly my view. Consider all of the issues that plague the security community, and ask yourself why a security professional who is overworked, nervous, and working under high expectations as BAU would take on another, ill-tested set of responsibilities when it's not even a requirement imposed by most employers. Well, they wouldn't would they?

Trending

Things are not all bad, though. DevSecOps has become mainstream. It is so fashionable that DevSecOps has become a pick-up line!

I was in a bar in Amsterdam having a chill-out afternoon with my business partner Stephen Ridgway and friend Chris Kubecka. A young man approached me, asked if he could sit down, and proceeded to compliment me (which was lovely, I mean he looked like a 20 year old Ed Sheeran so I didn't write home about it). He then said "I'm a DevSecOps Engineer, what do you do?" After I filled him in on what I do and what my company does he responded with, "Well, okay, I'm not actually a DevSecOps Engineer, I'm a DevSecOps Project Manager." I asked what his job entailed, (I was genuinely interested) and he then told me he was a DevSecOps

Intern and didn't really know what DevSecOps was. But he claimed, "It's all the rage!" before offering me his bong. It wasn't the most romantic situation, so, I must admit, I ended up leaving. It still makes me laugh that he thought "being a DevSecOps Engineer" was a good chat-up line. I really wanted to get that story into this book — it's a great example of DevSecOps being hyped up to such an exaggerated level that people use it as a chat-up line with women they have never met.

So After That Epic Moan, What Aspects of Security Does the SEC Need to Bring to DevSecOps?

We've all heard the expression "you can't see the wood for the trees." Well, threat modelling an application with little to no knowledge of offensive or defence security, especially if it's your own application, is inevitably going to leave holes. This should really be done by —or at least assisted by — a security teammate.

I don't believe as a security professional you need to be heavily engaged in writing code, but an interest in what developers in your organisation are working on, how the process works, and why they do things the way they do is certainly advantageous. Knowing how to test code for common vulnerabilities (not simply debugging, leave that to the devs) is where Sec adds value to DevSecOps.

Reviewing your own code and threat modelling your own application is like taking yourself to court to sue yourself. It's likely that a pen-tester will have a great deal more tricks to utilise in testing. It's great for a tester to sit with the developers upfront to correctly understand how the application is intended to be used. This is a great example of how DevSecOps can truly make a difference.

So is it all Fluff?

Do I think it's all fluff? No, no I certainly don't. DevSecOps is a reaction to what was, and still fundamentally is, a disjointed mix of technological fields. DevSecOps is a framework I'd encourage any company which produces technical products or relies heavily on developers to adopt. I'm simply asking you to question what and how you adopt it. I don't want to tell you what to think, I want to challenge you to please think. Let's ask the difficult questions, speak the truth, and get DevSecOps working for good.

About Eliza May Austin

Eliza May Austin is the CEO and Co-Founder of th4ts3cur1ty.company. The company specializes in delivering intelligence lead adversary emulation purple teaming, and the bespoke building of Security Operation Centers. Eliza is also the Founder and Director of Ladies of London Hacking Society, a passion project that has become one of London's leading technical security communities.

Acknowledgments

Did anyone actually read my whole rant? In that case I'd like to thank you for doing so. I'd like to thank Mark Miller and the team at DevSecOps Days for inviting me to contribute to this book. It is both jarring and flattering to be invited to co-exist in print with such talented and interesting people. I'd like to thank the proofreaders, who no doubt had a puzzling experience trying to fix my horrific grammar and sentencing issues. I honestly spell checked it but sometimes my spellings are so bad even Google gets confused.

REFERENCES

www.vanillaplus.com/2019/03/14/45749-businesses-open-security-risks-failing-integrate-DevSecOps-says-claranet-research

CHAPTER 2

Shift Left, Not S#!T Left

by Larry Maccherone

CHAPTER 2

Shift Left, Not S#!T Left

You can characterize the history of software engineering as an unending cycle of pendulum swings in search of a Goldilocks compromise that we never quite achieve. The Rational Unified Process (RUP) was people and process oriented, which was followed by Extreme Programming (XP) which was engineering oriented. Then, Agile took us back to people and process, followed by DevOps which is again more engineering focused.

Actually, there is a better analogy than the pendulum. Have you ever witnessed a first-time boat driver? A boat responds more slowly to steering input than the first-time boat driver expects, so their journey is a series of over-corrections, much like our Goldilocks-seeking pendulum swings. However, while the pendulum is always covering the same ground, the boat is constantly zig-zagging over new waters. That's the situation in software engineering. While RUP was about people and processes, its focus was on large organizations and the approach included the micro-definition of dozens of roles. Agile also has a lot to say about people and process, but more so, it is about product-market fit and its focus is on development teams you can feed with two pizzas. Also, it envisions only three roles, the Product Owner, the Scrum Master, and the Team, filled by "T-shaped" resources. Similarly, while both XP and DevOps address engineering practices, XP was more about code craftsmanship by a small number of developers, while DevOps, and especially its cousin, Site Reliability Engineering (SRE), has more to say about how a larger organization coordinates to build and operate larger systems.

Within each of these big movements are fractile layers of zig-zag. Agile encompasses Scrum, Crystal, SAFe, etc. Also, an interleaving third-order fractal occurs for the unique journey of each organization. This brings us to the focus of this chapter — the story of Comcast's journey towards DevSecOps. That journey was originally labeled with the phrase "shift left." However, those early efforts often felt more like, as Jeff Williams founder of OWASP and Contrast Security likes to say, "s#!t left" to the development teams whose behavior the initiative was seeking to change. Like the new boat driver, we had over-steered and had to learn from those early "epic failures" to get to the place we are now. Before I get into the details, let me first back up and set the stage.

Epic Failure Prelude: Bolt-On Application Security

The most fundamental epic failure is believing that you can sprinkle pixie dust on an already completed application to make it secure. This failure has been and continues to be widespread across the industry. When I started at Comcast, this was the general situation. Boundary protections like network firewalls as well as bolt-on solutions like web application firewalls were at the heart of our cybersecurity approach, despite the fact that the vast majority of security incidents were attributed to flaws in the underlying system design or software vulnerabilities.

I knew there was a better way because over a decade before I started at Comcast, I was part of an initiative to try to counter this bolt-on security mindset across the entire software development industry. At the time, I was the Software Assurance Director of Carnegie Mellon's CyLab. In that role, I co-led the launch of the Build-Security-In initiative along with industry thought-leader Gary McGraw, and Noopur Davis, a scientist at the Software Engineering Institute (also housed at Carnegie Mellon). However, we failed to significantly move the needle at the time. There were a number of headwinds that we were fighting.

» The security organization had the responsibility for security and thus the budget for change initiatives. Build-Security-In was all about getting development teams to take ownership of the problem but they didn't have the budget to do much.

» The lack of responsibility expected from development teams made it very hard to get them to change their behavior. "Why should we do more to ensure the security of our products? The security folks will take care of it, or at least tell us if we have to do anything ourselves."

» There is a profound lack of trust and thus little cooperation between security and development. Given the choice between an approach that requires influence over development team behavior and something they can do on their own, without the cooperation of the development team, the security group will choose the latter every time.

What a Difference a Decade Makes

The premature Build-Security-In initiative was not the first time in my career that I was too early to the party and it probably won't be the last, but a decade later, the situation was very different. The breakdown in the effectiveness of boundary protections had become painfully obvious. In 2013, an attacker bypassed the firewall at Target by exploiting a flaw in the HVAC system. <u>Once inside, the attackers easily found what they were looking for.</u>[1]

The Agile movement had broken down the silos between development, QA, and product management so that development teams felt empowered to take more ownership of the end-to-end delivery of value.

However, the real game-changer came in the form of the DevOps movement. DevOps gives both the motivation for security teams to change AND the means for development teams to take ownership. The motivation is driven by the fact that no amount of productivity improvement is going to enable throw-it-over-the-wall security specialist groups to keep up with the speed of DevOps teams; and DevOps automation is the means by which development teams can implement robust security validation in the CI/CD pipeline.

So, when Noopur Davis, my Build-Security-In co-founder, started her new job as CISO at Comcast, she asked me to join her and give our Build-Security-In idea another shot in this new fertile ground. That was almost four years ago and I believe we're in a great place now, but that doesn't mean we didn't have some epic failures along the way.

Epic Failure #1: Shifting Too Far Left Too Fast

If the goal of the initiative is to "shift security to the left," nothing is further left in the development cycle than providing vulnerability feedback as the developer is typing, right?

The first big push of our emerging DevSecOps initiative was to encourage the use of security scanning tools in the form of desktop scans and IDE plugins. Our tool selection effort prioritized this functionality highly. After an evaluation, selection, and a purchasing cycle, we were ready to start rolling it out. We went on a roadshow with the vendors to eight different locations where Comcast employs developers and gave our pitch to over 1,500 developers in the first round. We allocated expensive tool licenses to many of them but only got 190 developers to do an initial login and out of that 190 an even smaller number actually ran their first scan and only a handful got into a pattern of regular scanning.

We knew that we had to do better.

We looked at the few pockets of teams who were consistently running the scans. These teams had installed the scan as part of their team's CI/CD pipeline. They were interrupting the pipeline when the current pipeline run had vulnerabilities that exceeded the team's current policy threshold.

The surprising insight about these teams is that despite the fact that the scans were being run for them in their team's pipeline, they actually had the highest desktop scanning usage. Nobody wanted their code to be the reason the pipeline light turned red, so they were more inclined to check their work before submitting it to the pipeline.

We had shifted too far left too fast by expecting individual developers to change their behavior without the intermediate step of team-level reinforcement pro-vided by a CI/CD pipeline integration. You can think of this as a form of Chris Roberts', "*I* will fail. *We* will succeed."[2] You can also think of this as "s#!tting left" on the individual developers by expecting them to change behavior by their own willpower without giving them team-level reinforcement.

A related epic failure was that we chose tools that were optimized for desktop and IDE usage. Some of these tools also had great CI/CD integration and team-level functionality but not all of them so we had to change our tool mix.

LESSON A
A desktop scan is much more likely to occur when the developer knows that a team-level scan will be highly visible. Developer behavior is much easier to change when it's reinforced by highly visible team norms.

LESSON B
Optimize tool selection for those that enable rapid and easy integration into the CI/CD pipeline rather than IDE integration.

Epic Failure #2: Doing the Scans for the Team

We wanted to start steering the boat a little less to the left now. That meant our focus should shift to getting CI/CD pipeline scans going for each product before expecting developers to do desktop scans. So, we started brainstorming on ways to accomplish this. Just expecting individual teams to implement the scans themselves in the pipeline was going to be too inconsistent and sporadic. We decided to run a few experiments.

Like any large organization that has grown with acquisitions over the years, we have a number of relatively isolated parts of the organization each with a number of two-pizza development teams and each with their own local security directors and security specialists. Three of those groups volunteered to help pilot a more consistent approach to getting automated security scans. The idea was to identify the repositories where the source code was stored and run the scans for the individual two-pizza teams in a pipeline that a cybersecurity group maintained. We had three completely different results from the three experiments.

1. The smallest org had only five development teams and they had by far the most success with this approach. However, when we looked at why, it became obvious that the success was partially a function of the relatively small size of the organization combined with the superpowers of that local security director. She made sure her teams got near-immediate feedback on the scan results and she had a knack for cajoling the teams all the way to resolution of the findings. This success was going to be hard to duplicate in larger orgs even in the unlikely event we could find each a local director with similar superpowers, and the vast majority of the rest of Comcast development teams had no such local security director or specialists.

We weren't going to mess with the success of this group but at the same time, we didn't think it was a good approach to apply more broadly. This reluctance was reinforced by the fact that our larger central cybersecurity group often complained that 60-80% of their time was spent cajoling reluctant development teams.

2. The largest org also had the largest staff of security specialists and dedicated project management resources. They quickly came up with a project plan to get scans running for the 150 or so applications in their org. They got management to put scan coverage metrics on their team's quarterly goals, and they started executing the plan.

This rollout was about 30% done when we noticed a huge problem. While the scans were being run consistently, negative findings had essentially zero resolution. Comcast gets almost no value out of knowing exactly how many vulnerabilities we have. The scale for the information value of such data is 0, a few, and many. More information than that is just gilding. The real value only comes from the risk reduction of removing vulnerabilities from our products. We needed the scans to drive the rapid resolution of the findings and we weren't seeing that. We immediately put the brakes on the rollout plan, a more difficult task than you might imagine considering the rewards associated with the achievement of pre-set quarterly goals, but we controlled the licenses so we eventually got them to listen.

We told them that the license spigot would not be turned back on until we started to see a healthy resolution curve. They shifted most of their local security specialist resources towards resolution of scan findings. This involved cajoling individual teams with whom they had about as good a relationship as the central cybersecurity group did with their development teams. We started to see a shallow resolution curve but cajoling was taking up 60-80% of their effort. It was too little result from too much effort. Perhaps more telling was the fact that the folks in that local security specialist group were not enjoying this cajoling work. One described it as "soul-crushing." A few of them left and more threatened. This sub-org was recently subject to a reorg and it is yet to be seen if that will lead to improvement or make this problem worse.

We were left with no choice but to conclude that this too was not a sustainable, repeatable approach. In fact, it felt very similar to the bolt-on, throw-it-over-the-wall, prelude-epic-failure that we started with. The only distinction was that the scans were automatically run on a more frequent cadence rather than occasionally run by a security specialist's hand. It was a distinction without a difference.

3. The third group was our proverbial Goldilocks "just right." Rather than stand up an out-of-band CI/CD pipeline, they integrated the cybersecurity scanning tools into their org-level-maintained CI/CD tool as a template that could be applied to projects. This meant that the feedback came to the team in the exact same form as other failing tests.

A vulnerability became just a kind of defect. Resolving them became just another aspect of their low-defect mindset. After the initial set of findings were burned down, teams stayed at zero vulnerabilities.

While experiment #3 provided a model for us to repeat, org-level centralization experiment #2 is an example of steering the boat too far back to the right as an overcorrection to our too far left to fast EPIC FAILURE #1. For experiment #2 above, we were s#!tting left upon our org-local cybersecurity groups by expecting them to drive resolution without a good model for how to do that. Centralizing around an independent pipeline rather than plugging into the team's own pipeline was a big mistake because it meant that feedback was out-of-band which in turn meant that cajoling the resolution of findings became a huge slog.

LESSON C

Rather than stand up an independent pipeline, create recipes and templates to enable easy CI/CD integration of cybersecurity scanning tools into the team's existing pipeline and defect resolution process so vulnerability feedback is responded to like any other defect feedback.

LESSON D

Insist that the development team own the problem of security for their product and accept that security's role is not one of gatekeeper, but rather tool smith and advisor.

LESSON E

Create a culture where it's more important to do the right thing at all times even if that means someone will miss their quarterly metric goals. This might mean you have to get a policy changed, an exception issued, or go up against the boss or the legal department.

Epic Failure #3: DevSecOps Without DevOps

While the experiments described in the last section were underway, the rest of my team was continuing to do white glove pipeline integration of our evolving suite of security scanning tools. Whenever we found a team that was really using their CI/CD tooling, we had similar success as experiment #3 above in terms of relatively rapid resolution of findings, however, there were a number of problems that became obvious.

» Less than half of the teams we were working with at the time were serious about their use of CI/CD tools.

» There were about a dozen different CI/CD tools in use around the company and no single tool had more than 18% internal market share.

» The most common pattern was for each team to stand up their own CI/CD tool which meant they were inconsistently configured often with wide-open ports, unpatched servers, and no access control thus adding to the cyber-security risk as opposed to reducing it. Via port scanning, we were able to determine that there were over 100 different Jenkins servers on our network. We would have to visit each of them to do this right.

» Since there was no central well-supported CI/CD tooling, our ability to follow Lesson C which says to focus on central recipes and templates, was much harder. That was a lot more work to do for 12 CI/CD tools than it would have been to do for one or even a few.

» When we came across teams with immature DevOps practices, there was no group to whom we could refer them to improve their DevOps practices. We filled in where we could but it wasn't our mandate.

This wasn't going to scale and I started telling my management that the lack of DevOps maturity in the organization was the most serious limiting factor. We could get less mature teams to submit their applications for pen testing and threat modeling. We could continue our rollout of ever-improving cybersecurity training, but we could never achieve the high levels of quality and security with automation that we were able to accomplish with high maturity teams.

When any of my staff had to work with these not-quite-DevOps teams, they were disappointed because they knew how much easier and more effective our efforts would be if they'd only had a CI/CD pipeline.

In the spirit of not letting a good crisis go to waste, Noopur and I put the growing influence of our DevSecOps program behind an ongoing effort to standardize as much as possible around a well-supported multi-tenant CI/CD tool and DevOps practice adoption initiative. We helped write the budget proposal and we built first-class support for the chosen CI/CD tool in the form of reusable resources that any team could add to their pipeline with a few lines of YAML. We now have a multi-million dollar per year DevOps transformation program that keeps our multi-tenant CI/CD tools up and running and is assisting development teams with white-glove pipeline implementations very similar to our own. Teams who have onboarded to that DevOps program now have a robust base upon which to implement our security scanning tools and practices. Such teams are now fast tracked through our DevSecOps program.

LESSON F

Create different tracks for different team personas. Fast track those with mature DevOps practices. Invest the bare minimum to provide traditional application security support for teams with lower DevOps maturity, but insist that they get on the path to DevOps maturity before you do more... and connect those teams with the right group to start on this DevOps journey.

Epic Failure #4: DevOps/DevSecOps Without Pull Requests

Pull requests (aka "merge requests" in the lingo of some GitHub competitors) are an elegant way for the work of an individual developer to be merged into the product. Open source has been using pull requests for a long time but now almost all software development even inside large organizations is moving towards using them for everything. Having used them for all of my own team's development, we were always aware of the value of pull requests, but as we started working with teams at Comcast, we noticed that there was an almost perfect correlation between the use of pull requests and their success or failure with DevOps or DevSecOps. With this data, our recommendation grew to insistence which provided several benefits.

» The pull request can be configured to require a code review by another member of the team, who with a bit of training, can look for security issues that tools are not good at finding. This "security peer review" is another one of our recommended DevSecOps practices that is easy to adopt by teams that are already doing quality-oriented peer review as part of their pull request practice.

» The pull request provides a central place where all feedback can be made visible and recorded for later reference. The CI/CD tool provides a similar place for visibility and record-keeping but it will be missing code reviews and other forms of feedback. We have teams that use one CI/CD instance for building and testing and a different instance for deploying. Other teams use SaaS services for purposes like test coverage visualization, accessibility testing, DAST, etc., that are separate from their CI/CD pipeline, although often triggered by the same GitHub event. You can aggregate the output of all such feedback in the pull request.

» However, the biggest advantage of pull requests centers around developer psychology. Every developer wants their code to get into the product as soon as possible. Developers care a lot about the code they wrote this morning and will respond to any feedback preventing that from happening... including vulnerabilities found by security scanning tools.

The subplot in this section didn't involve oversteering like the other sections, but rather, we realized that we were understeering and would benefit by steering further left in this regard.

This ties in nicely to the story I told earlier about the sub-org in Epic Failure #2, Experiment #2. Once we steered our DevSecOps initiative hard towards pull requests it became part of our coaching practice. I was leading a coaching session for the org-local cybersecurity team for that sub-org when the cybersecurity leader told me that my approach wouldn't work because he didn't think the teams in his org used pull requests, although he was uncertain what a pull request was. One of that leader's direct reports corrected him on the spot saying that many of their client teams were in fact using them and at least one had explicitly asked for the scan results to tie into them.

The desire to get out of the "soul crushing" cajoling role was at war with this org-local cybersecurity team's unwillingness to relinquish some control and trust the development team to own the security of their products. It is still to be seen if they will steer further left in this way but we now have them thinking about it, and they know that the rest of the organization is steering further left.

LESSON G
If you don't know what a pull request is, LEARN, and then encourage all teams to use them for all code that needs to be merged into the product. Make sure the feedback from every cybersecurity scanning tool shows up in the status checks for the pull request.

Epic Failure #5: Insisting on a Cybersecurity Practice Before You've Implemented the Easy Button for That Practice

Like many organizations, our cybersecurity policies were a bit aspirational. They were cobbled together from a myriad of competing industry standards and never validated with real-world development. When I started, we wanted to identify a small set of practices that every team should be able to do and insist upon every single team complying. One such practice was a requirement that no secrets (passwords, certificates, etc.) be stored in source code repositories. However, the first few teams we met with said, "OK, we understand why you don't want secrets in source code repositories. Where should we put them?" We didn't have a great answer. We could point to one other team that had stood up their own secrets vault and others who had homegrown solutions, but there was no "click here to get started with our standard secrets vault."

Talk about s#!tting left.

So, we steered the boat right and temporarily took secrets management out of our shortlist of critical practices while we stood up robust self-service support for our chosen secrets vault. Then we steered left again and started expecting all teams to stop storing secrets in source code repositories.

LESSON H
Make it "click here to get started" easy before you insist that teams comply with a particular policy.

Epic Failure #6: Lack of Trust Between Security and Development

About three weeks after I started at Comcast, I was describing the lack of trust between security and development to my executive leadership as a major obstacle for my mission. One of the executives in the room asked, "What are we supposed to do about it? It's not as if trust is a formula." It reminded me of something that I'd learned earlier in my career. I have an entire blog series on the Trust Algorithm for DevSecOps up on the DevSecOpsDays[3] website so I won't press the point except to describe the problem and tease the solution. Maybe this sounds familiar...

Security people: "Those darn developers are cranking out crap that's going to get us hacked!"

Developers: "Security is nothing but an obstacle. They don't understand that we have lots of other concerns and the only 'help' they provide is to browbeat us."

The solution goes like this:

THE TRUST ALGORITHM

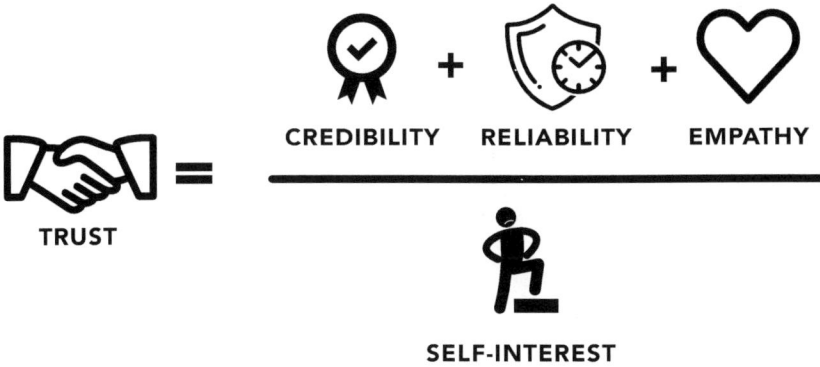

$$\text{TRUST} = \frac{\text{CREDIBILITY} + \text{RELIABILITY} + \text{EMPATHY}}{\text{SELF-INTEREST}}$$

Where:

> » **Credibility** = How well you actually know what you are talking about

> » **Reliability** = How often and quickly do you do what you say

> » **Empathy** = How much you show that you care about someone else's interests

> » **Apparent Self-Interest** = How apparent it is that your words and actions are in your own interest

I have been using some form of the above formula since someone I worked with at Rally Software shared something similar with me. Until recently, I didn't know where it originally came from but I've since learned that it's the original work of Charlie Green at TrustedAdvisor.[4] Many thanks after the fact to Charlie.

While this part of the story doesn't involve any oversteering, it definitely is an example of how slow it is to turn a boat. Also, it is a form of s#!tting left ironically by not trusting the folks we should be shifting left towards. The boat has turned and we now see much higher levels of trust going both ways.

LESSON I
Build trust between security and development by following the Trust Algorithm (shameless plug).

"Who Moved My Cheese?" Deja-Vu

Maybe it's no surprise, considering the Agile transformation background of our CISO and myself, but the approach I've described in this chapter borrows much from successful Agile transformation approaches. It's heavy on team-level ownership and empowerment with the minimum structure to assure high-level alignment. Shifting, rather than s#!tting, left means that the security group must change their role from gatekeeping and policy enforcement to a role of coaching and tool-smithing.

I've been telling this Agile-transformation-like DevSecOps story at conferences for the last couple of years. In candid moments after my talk (usually over adult beverages at the conference reception), my approach is sometimes dismissed as naive kumbaya... or more politely with something like, "That sounds like it's great for you but it'll never work at our organization because ‹something that indicates a lack of trust in development teams›."

These are deja-vu moments for me because they are the exact same reaction I got from software quality assurance (QA) leaders after my talks at the beginning of the Agile movement.

The Agile movement involved breaking down silos and moving the responsibility for quality and product management to the development team. At the beginning of the Agile movement, the QA folks refused to believe that the development team could ever be trusted to confirm the quality of their products and that a separate QA organization would always be necessary. Fast forward 15 years to now — very few organizations still have a dedicated QA department. The folks formerly employed by those departments either learned to code and joined a development team as "T-shaped resources" with QA as the vertical part of the "T," or they found another job. Similarly, with the DevOps movement, dedicated operations departments are being evolved into site reliability engineering (SRE) teams and/or more and more of their responsibility is being shifted to DevOps teams.

Another aspect of the current Dev[Sec]Ops movement that reminds me of the old QA/Agile story is around automation. When developers took ownership of QA, they automated previously manual testing. With the DevOps movement, developers are taking ownership of how their products behave in production and they are automating all deployment and operations tasks. Security is joining the party with the start of the DevSecOps sub-movement and security specialists will need to pick up CI/CD automation experience to stay relevant.

I'm reminded of a book, "Who Moved My Cheese?" that's often given to about-to-be-let-go employees whose skills and mindset have become obsolete. It's a story about two mice. One who quickly adjusts to the changing environment when his cheese is moved, and another who stagnates in place for a long time after. The DevSecOps movement of today is at roughly the same place that the Agile movement was 15 years ago and the DevOps movement was 3-5 years ago.

This time security specialists are the ones whose cheese is about to be moved. You can either dismiss what I'm saying as kumbaya that is not relevant to your organization or you can start to get yourself and your organization ready for this emerging DevSecOps movement.

About Larry Maccherone

Larry Maccherone is an industry-recognized thought leader on DevSecOps, Lean/Agile, and Analytics. He currently leads the DevSecOps transformation at Comcast. Previously, Larry led the Insights product line at Rally Software where he published the largest ever study correlating development team practices with performance. Before Rally, Larry worked at Carnegie Mellon with the Software Engineering Institute (SEI) and CyLab for seven years conducting research on cybersecurity and software engineering. While there, he co-led the launch of the DHS-funded Build-Security-In initiative. He has also served as Principal Investigator for the NSA's Code Assessment Methodology Project, on the Advisory Board for IARPA's STONESOUP program, and as the Department of Energy's Los Alamos National Labs Fellow.

Contact Larry via his LinkedIn page: www.linkedin.com/in/LarryMaccherone.

REFERENCES

1. www.zdnet.com/article/anatomy-of-the-target-data-breach-missed-opportunities-and-lessons-learned

2. www.devsecopsdays.com/articles/epic-failures-in-devsecops-book-download

3. www.devsecopsdays.com/articles/trust-algorithm-applied-to-devsecops

4. trustedadvisor.com/articles/the-trust-equation-a-primer

CHAPTER 3

Making Everyone Visible in Tech

by Jaclyn Damiano

CHAPTER 3

Making Everyone Visible in Tech

Here's a past I don't talk about often. I grew up in a small-ish (77K population) coal-mining town. When the mines closed, the service sector became the primary source of employment in the community. My family didn't have a lot, but we had what we needed. My mom and dad, divorced, both worked. Before and after school and during the summers, we couldn't afford daycare, so I would spend time with my grandparents in the housing project where my parents grew up. I threw myself into school, that was my outlet. I love learning and I love the feeling of achievement, school provided me with both, and luckily so has my career. I've worked in tech and finance for the past eighteen years at some amazing companies. I'm no stranger to being the only woman in the room. As I've gotten older and more senior (and certainly grayer), I've started to feel like the tech industry is getting less and less diverse.

The research supports this: Ryan Carson, CEO of Treehouse, says: "Most companies have a significant challenge recruiting and retaining a diverse set of employees, particularly women in technology. For our team to match the diversity of America, we'd need 13.4% Black, 1.3% Native American, 18.1% Latinx, and 50% women employees. " Today, 7% of the high tech sector workforce is Black, and 8% is Hispanic. Depending on what source you read, between 20-36% of the high tech sector is female. Most research also states only 18% of engineering graduates are female. The problem intensifies as you look up the hierarchy. In the U.S. top 1,000 companies by revenue, only 19% of CIOs are women.

Those of us who work in tech need only to look around during a meeting to be confronted with an all-too-real illustration of these numbers. Sometimes I look around an office building and check out the conference rooms. Who is sitting around the table? If I see only men, I have an odd compulsion to run into the room screaming "Wait, you're missing a gender!" Gender is only the beginning of what it means to have a diverse team.

The research on diversity is clear: Diversity isn't just about being nice or noble. Diverse teams build better products, which increase company revenue. In today's economy, companies cannot afford to develop products with a provincial mindset. Many of us are committed to changing this situation, we truly understand that it is imperative to better reflect the perspectives of our diverse customer bases. However, even with all of our good intentions, our industry has had a really hard time creating and implementing a plan to increase diversity in technology.

Eighteen months ago, I was quietly lamenting this issue. Then something happened that completely changed my career, and honestly my life. An epic failure occurred on the team I lead.

At my company, one of the teams I lead hosts a Tech Day three times a year. These Tech Days mimic a DevOps Day format. We bring in external luminaries to speak, and we ask our internal employees to speak and share their stories of successes and failures. These events have two distinct goals, building community and energizing our engineers. In mid-2018, we sent out a Call For Papers (CFP) to 1,000 engineers. Guess how many women responded to this call?

Well, if you guessed zero (or you've heard me previously bellow about this during a public talk), you're right. We failed. We failed to have a diverse agenda.

How Did We Get Here?

I had one reaction: WTF? How could this happen with me at the helm? I am a feminist. I want women to be on stage, telling their stories. What the hell is going on? I'm missing an entire gender of speakers. So, I started to do research. And, I'm ashamed to say, I learned things that I should've known long ago.

» **The Confidence Gap:** Katy Kay & Claire Shipman from *The Atlantic* wrote, "In studies, men overestimate their abilities and performance, and women underestimate both. Their performances do not differ in quality."

» **The Bravery Deficit:** Reshma Saujani, Founder & CEO of Girls Who Code, worries about society "raising our girls to be perfect and our boys to be brave." Her point is so spot on. If we don't encourage our girls to take risks, climb the tree, and fall, they'll never experience failure and recovery, a critical skill in business.

» **Women fail because they don't begin:** *Harvard Business Review* published a study stating: "Men apply to jobs if they meet 60% of the qualifications. Women apply for jobs only if they meet 100% of the qualifications." Frighteningly, statistics are similar when it comes to promotions.

Why don't we see women in the workplace? Another *Harvard Business Review* article, "Why Women Stay Out of the Spotlight at Work," states that women stay out of the spotlight for three main reasons: avoiding backlash in the workplace, finding professional authenticity, and parenthood pressures. In other words, women are afraid of being called out as bitchy; *HBR* states "Most women rejected the executive, self-promoting leadership style in favor of a mission-oriented, communal style." And, balancing parenthood and working is freaking hard.

I learned a lot through my research that helped me understand more about myself, which was great. However, what I learned didn't solve my problem at work. I still had a hard time getting women to volunteer to speak. So, I did the only thing I thought would help: I turned our failure of having a male-driven agenda and my subsequent research into a talk. I added some tactical things that everyone can do to help mitigate the situations outlined above:

» Women need to sit at the table during a meeting. Do not call in, do not sit along the perimeter of the room. Claim your voice. If you absolutely need to be remote, make sure you share your expertise, don't stay quiet.

» Women need to be wary of volunteering for "unpromotable tasks." Let someone else plan the next team event; potlucks will not get you promoted.

» Women need to help each other. Introduce yourself, be there for someone else coming up the chain.

» Women need to speak at conferences. Please, for the love of God, having any conference be one of anything is super boring.

» Men, start nudging your female colleagues to share their stories.

» People Leaders: Be a critic. Be a coach. Be a cheerleader. Try to be all three to the same person. The results will amaze you.

At our next Tech Day, I gave this talk in an ignite style. I called it "Making Women Visible" and delivered it in September-ish 2018. As it happened, during this particular DevOps Day, one of our external luminaries was Dominica DeGrandis, a personal hero of mine. Her book, "Making Work Visible," is required reading for anyone on my team, and obviously, my talk title was a riff on her book title. She complimented me on my talk and encouraged me to keep speaking.

And Then, a Woman Gave Another Woman a Voice

Fast forward a few weeks — there was a last-minute opening at the upcoming 2018 DevOps Enterprise Summit (DOES) in Las Vegas for the Ignite section. Dominica reached out and told me to just say "yes" to fill the spot. Before I could second guess myself, I typed those three letters.

In October of 2018, I gave my Ignite — Where Are All The IT Women? — at the DevOps Enterprise Summit. The response was overwhelming. People were cheering as I spoke, when I got off the stage, Gene Kim hugged me. I mean it was surreal. After the talk, woman after woman approached me, thanking me for talking about the issues we "deal" with but don't speak about. Some women cried. Men approached me asking how they could help their teammates, sisters, kids, etc. I was overwhelmed. I felt elated, of course, but I also felt "it" creeping in, a sense of responsibility to help change these conditions. But who am I to try to fix this massive issue? I'm not a diversity and inclusion expert. I'm only a believer in this stuff, I'm not a teacher.

Then, two days later, our team flew home from DOES. As our plane landed in Newark my mentor and boss at the time looked at me and said "That talk really resonated with people. So what are you going to do about it? The community is looking to you." Oh, dear God. I could either do something about this, or I could just keep talking about it, perpetuating inaction. I'm here writing a chapter, so you could probably guess that I have a bias for action...

Think! You Need A Plan. . . A Good One.

In the coming days, I thought a lot about what I could do that would make a meaningful impact. I might be able to increase female representation at our Tech Days, but that would be a temporary and localized win. How would little old me be a part of the solution to further diversity tech?

Then like magic, the light bulb went on. I was at the Grace Hopper Celebration in 2018. Mariana Costa-Chica, who formed an organization called Laboratoria in South America, was honored for her work in diversifying tech. There weren't enough women in tech in Peru, so she went out to underserved communities to find women who had not just a passion for technology, but had the aptitude to make a great developer. She brought successful candidates into a boot camp and trained them how to code. Her results are undeniably successful:

» 1,300+ graduates in 5 years

» 76% placement rate in companies like Accenture and Thoughtworks

» 3x income growth for graduates employed

Her talk resonated with me because of where I grew up. I didn't know what a software engineer was until I went to college. And we all know...

If You Can't See It, You Can't Become It

I never had anyone in my life that was in technology. I didn't know what corporate America was, outside of my mom's job. She worked at the Yellow Pages as a graphic designer and dressed nicely to go to her desk job. She worked so hard and gave up so many things so we could have what we needed. My dad, one of the smartest people I know, worked in a machine shop for a decent part of my childhood, and then for the government (he now has a master's degree). I worked hard in school because the results felt good. Then before I knew it, I was in my junior year of high school, and my dad mentioned to me an article in the New York Times that covered Bucknell University. A year later I was accepted.

Bucknell changed my life. I met friends that made me feel safe and accepted. I studied topics that were interesting and engaging. I took my first economics class and discovered this was the lens through which the world made sense to me. (My friend Emily explained that this is how I'd "know" my major when I found it. She was eternally right. Now she's an astrophysicist.) In any case, I fit at Bucknell, academically.

Socioeconomically, well that was a different story. Many of my classmates were wealthy, so well dressed, so beautiful, so smart, and so refined. I would see the J.Crew boxes come and go in the mailroom. My first job in college was in the cafeteria, wearing a hairnet and making pizzas (yes, I know Adam Sandler's Lunch Lady song, I like to think that was an ode to me). Luckily, I found an office job on campus quickly. Regardless of my own inferiority complex, I managed to graduate with a 3.46 GPA. I am a first generation college graduate. I still lament that I didn't graduate with honors. I still can't believe they didn't round. Anyway, off to New York City.

Why am I divulging all of this to you, dear reader? A couple of reasons. First, I have a fear that someone may think I'm a privileged person who has a savior complex. I worry that people think that I am going into communities that I feel sorry for, trying to save them. As fortunate as it is that I'm on this side of the story, I feel like I could have easily been one of the people that Mariana helped lift up. Second, some people get squeamish when I talk about working alongside people who didn't go to college or who may not have ever had a role model who worked in an office. It's at these points in conversations that I've started to have to speak up and tell them about where and how I grew up.

In summary — at the end of the day, I have a responsibility to do what I can to give others a chance. To give people an opportunity. There are too many smart people in crappy situations that need a door. They'll walk through that door if they want it — trust me, I've seen it.

So, What's Stopping Me From Running A Program Like Laboratoria in the U.S., at My Company?

Apparently nothing. Nothing except money and sign off. No biggie, right? I drew up a plan that looked similar to Mariana's program...

» Find a diverse set of applicants from underserved communities that have underlying skills that will make them great developers. The barriers to entry in the technology field are low, according to Stack Overflow's developer survey, 17% of developers do not have an associate's or bachelor's degree. 25% of those who have graduated from college and are working in tech have a degree outside of Computer Engineering/Software Development. Given this, we believe we can establish an apprenticeship program that can create solid entry level developers from a pool of people with limited to no technical experience.

» Bring the apprentices in and pay them a living wage during their learning.

» Co-locate the apprentices and teach them how to code. Use multiple modalities of instruction: online, in-person, 1:1, and group coaching. Eventually, deploy apprentices to line-of-business technical teams to code in the company's repositories.

» Provide apprentices opportunities to apply for full-time employment at our company.

Now, when I talk about diversity, I realize it's not just about gender and race. It's about a lot of things: socioeconomic status, religion, age, body size/shape, sexual orientation, people with different abilities, cognitive differences, etc. The list goes on and is deep and broad. When it was time to put a call out for applicants, we marketed to all people in hopes that we'd end up with a diverse set of candidates. It worked. Our apprentices are all different, brilliant human beings who ended up, in large part, becoming awesome engineers. More on that later.

"This Is No Time To Be Chickenshit, Frances."

—Under The Tuscan Sun

I needed money and headcount to get this program running. I called it Project Athena (yes, the Goddess of Math, I've had enough of "Project Hercules"); my brief experience leading a marketing and communications team taught me how important it was to brand this project. Simply stated, the goal of Athena is to enable people from underserved and underrepresented communities to grow into awesome technologists to build products our customers love. Project Athena provides an actionable plan to create a new labor pipeline of qualified, diverse people to work in technology.

I put the idea on paper, and by mid-November 2018, I was pitching it to my boss. I expected him to say it was crazy. The idea was too big. It wasn't the right time. It was too expensive. Instead, he said, "this is a good idea." Excuse me, what? Nope. It's not too expensive. Yep. It is the right time. The idea was big but good. Wow.

During this time, my company was going through some major changes. Selling a plan like this is hard; selling it when things are changing was harder. These changes, though, presented a great opportunity. We had to hire a lot of people in a short amount of time. Ever spin up a job requisition in tech? Finding the right candidate can take months. Finding many right candidates all at once is super difficult. If we had a program to create a talent pipeline where it did not exist, that would help. We can train them how we want them, and then plant them as seeds of change in our organization.

After my boss encouraged me, I got on our senior vice president's calendar. I was waiting for him to kill the idea. But he didn't. He thought it was a good one. He scheduled a meeting with our CIOs in January. I created a pitch deck, outlining the costs and benefits. I told them how I thought this could help with our open requisitions, and how we could diversify our staff. They listened. They asked lots of questions. They asked me to work with HR and get alignment. I was terrified. I had no relationship with our HR leader, and I knew that this was an "outside the box" program that would require a leap of faith. At large enterprises, we have a lot of responsibilities, and sometimes we get too afraid to jump. On top of that, some HR employees may construe this kind of activity to be a threat to their role in talent acquisition. I'm happy to report my HR partners jumped with me, and were enormously supportive. They kept me sane (and employed) during this project. Jeepers, the things they deal with! We have it easy with systems. They're dealing with the most complex system ever created: people. Respect.

In January, I also took the stage in NYC at a public DevOps Days event. I proposed Project Athena to the audience. At the time, I wasn't sure my company would approve the initiative. I wanted to get an external read on how it would play. The result was one that I've come to rely on from this community: nothing but love and support.

Between January and March of 2019, I met with anyone at my company that would talk to me about Project Athena, hundreds of people. I reached out to wildly senior people (C-Level, the board of directors) in my organization to pitch the idea. I learned something super important: The busiest, most senior people always make the time to talk to people. I remember crying when I got a note back from one of the senior most executives in our company, expressing his support for the program. I mean, he's a genius and he took the time to respond to me? A girl from Scranton who worked in the cafeteria during college? How'd it come to be that I had a voice someone was interested in hearing? It's moments like these that I hear *Panic! At The Disco* running through my head: "Hey look, ma, I made it..." It's just an email, woman. Get it together. I will tell you, through this period of time I thought the program was dead about a dozen times. Jennifer Wood from London DOES 2019 talked about the "abyss of despair." Man, I was in that abyss a lot during this pitch period, but, as Jennifer points out, things always turn around. Whenever I put the plan aside because I was discouraged, I'd get a call or a meeting or a word of encouragement that made me pick it back up. Finally, it was time to get a go/no-go on this thing.

I Needed Our CIO To Green Light This

In March 2019, I met with my CIO to ask for his permission to begin the program. He said yes on two conditions: 1. I needed to source the headcount from each of the other CIOs myself, and 2. I needed to ensure that the passion I had for this project was shared by other people in the organization. I sent an email to our CIO leader teams asking for headcount and a representative from their team who was passionate about diversity. Each CIO showed up. They committed headcount to the proposal and an advocate from their organization. I had the green light. We signed an agreement with a partner to help us make connections with organizations in underserved areas that would help us source the right candidates.

In April 2019, we started recruiting. We decided to recruit 40 people, thinking we'd have a 50% attrition rate through the program. Our requirements for past experience? Applicants needed to have a high school degree or equivalent. We partnered with Workforce Solutions in Texas and New Jersey. We also partnered with the Salvation Army in Texas. 400 people initially applied to our program. They then went through an online technology course and completed an essay-based application. We selected the top 40 candidates, 20 in each location.

I'm going to pause here and talk about the enormous lift my team made between April and May. We had to run all language about the program through HR and Legal, application forms and job descriptions. We had to learn the onboarding process and get 40 people through things like background checks within a short amount of time. We needed to get 40 computers, logins and badges. We had last minute paperwork issues. Who is funding this? What is the budget code? The what? I promise, I couldn't believe the power of a one-word email from my SVP "Approved." He later told me he just needed to give me sign-offs and then get out of my way. I'll never forget that. It's a sign of a true leader. Trust your people. Give them the support they need, then get out of their way.

Onboarding one person in any company is usually difficult. Imagine 40 at once. My Dojo operations gurus handled this with grace and poise. I also have to stop and say, sometimes at large companies we get in our own way. But jeepers, when we all believe in something, it moves, and it moves fast. I have buddies in HR, Finance, and Legal who are now my village. They believed in Athena. They moved mountains for us.

It Really Happened

During the last week of May, we had our orientation/kick-off celebration and all of our apprentices joined us on site. I was numb. I expected to be elated. I think I was partially paralyzed with fear. What were we doing? What if this failed? We immediately needed to put all of our self doubt aside. On our first day in Texas, we realized that our apprentices had needs we weren't anticipating. Some of our apprentices were facing Maslow's Hierarchy of Needs issues. We had a few people who were houseless. More were food insecure. Some didn't have cars. It was at this moment we realized this work wasn't just work, it was, as one of my CIOs would call it, noble work. Few of us on staff had dealt with these issues. We did the best we could, but most of the time we were figuring it out as we went along. We created food drawers in each location that the apprentices had access to for nourishment. We tried to come up with solutions to seemingly intractable problems (bus rides three hours each way to the office, medications that could only be distributed at the shelter during work hours, etc.), when the apprentices just needed someone to listen. It's not a stretch to say we learned more from them than they did from us.

On June 3rd, we co-located these candidates in our Dojos. Dojos are immersive learning centers, permanent physical spaces where onsite coaches work with employee teams to upskill. A full stack team comes into the Dojo with their backlog, and we work with them to do product discovery and teach them modern engineering practices. We leveraged our Dojo model, and assigned coaches to apprentices at a 1:10 ratio. The apprentices spent most of their day learning from a full-stack JavaScript online curriculum especially designed for people with no background in tech. This learning was augmented significantly by the coaches. The coaches did weekly 1:1s with each apprentice. By talking the coaches through the apprentices' code, the coaches could get a good understanding of where the apprentices needed extra help. The coaches would then do reinforcement learning sessions, Katas, etc. They were working night and day to stay ahead of the apprentices in the curriculum.

The Dojo learning continued through the end of September. At this point, we wanted the apprentices to be placed in line-of-business technology to get their hands dirty with real coding repositories. We held a job fair, and made apprentice placements. The Dojo felt lonely again. The coaches supported the apprentices while they were working with the teams.

In November, we posted junior developer jobs. Our apprentices applied and interviewed for these positions. I'm happy to say that 80% of our apprentices are converting to full-time employees.

What We Learned

Holy creepers! We are responsible for the livelihood of 40 people. We weren't used to working in an environment where someone's life depended on what we did. This was the first time many of my staff saw the realities of poverty. It was also the first time many of them couldn't "fix" something. We all learned that sometimes what we needed to do was just listen, because fixing it wasn't something we could do.

Crying is okay. Even at work. Even if you're typically a tough chick or dude. Before Athena, I had only cried at work three times during 18 years. Now we have a joke in the Dojo that we cry weekly. Tears of joy and frustration, all of the feelings.

Not knowing what is coming next sucks, but #itsgonnabefine. More often than not, we had no idea how the heck we were going to get 40 people with no tech background to be beginner developers in six months. We didn't know SO much. But what I did know, what experience has taught me, is that very few things are not fixable. My team will tell you that whenever we faced a big challenge, the words that would come across my lips were "it's gonna be fine." Because, honestly, it had to be. In October of 2019, #itsgonnabefine became a laptop sticker for the staff and me. Because we were braver, we were stronger and we knew we could do this.

We did more good than harm. We were super self critical throughout the program. Could we teach more effectively? Could we give them more support? 10% of our original apprentices dropped out of the apprenticeship. We couldn't make it work for everyone. However, it did work for the 36 people who graduated from the program and now had an experience working in IT in a large enterprise. 80% of the 36 graduates converted to full-time employment at our company. I like to think that we've changed the lives of those people and their children.

There's some irony in my story. Here I am trying to help educate women about feeling like an imposter, like somehow they don't deserve to be successful yet how many times in this narrative did my insecurities come out? Once you see it in black and white, it cannot be unseen. I try to carry that with me. I am more educated now, but not immune to falling victim to the confidence gap.

What's Next?

We have funding for another cohort in 2020. We are looking at how to self-fund through governmental grants specifically earmarked for software development apprenticeships. We are also considering what other areas of our company we can use apprenticeship as a viable model.

About Jaclyn Damiano

Jaclyn is an Associate Director at one of the world's leading telecommunications companies. Jacki leads enterprise wide initiatives aimed at creating a culture that passionately embraces modern engineering and organizational practices. Previously, Jacki held roles as a business analyst and project manager at Accenture, AllianceBernstein, and Goldman Sachs. Her passions include Product Management, Enabling Cultural Change at Scale, and Diversity and Inclusion. Jacki is an active member of the DevOps community and regularly delivers talks on digital transformation and diversity at tech conferences. She proudly earned her B.A. in Economics from Bucknell University.

Acknowledgments

Mark, thank you for the honor of contributing to this book — I am so grateful to know you! Also, thank you to the editors and everyone who made sense of my writing. Most of all, thanks to my kids and husband who support (most of) my crazy ideas.

REFERENCES

» hbr.org/2018/11/how-my-company-created-an-apprenticeship-program-to-help-diversify-tech
» www.techrepublic.com/article/5-eye-opening-statistics-about-minorities-in-tech
» www.cio.com/article/3267945/deloitte-report-has-some-good-news-about-women-in-technology.html
» www.mckinsey.com/business-functions/organization/our-insights/why-diversity-matters

DEV
SEC
OPS
DAYS

CHAPTER 4

From Silos to Communities

*by Sladjana Jovanovic
and
Bill McArthur*

CHAPTER 4

From Silos to Communities

As humans we have evolved through living in tribes. Look around you, we are social beings and we feel most comfortable within our own tribe. We truly believe that our tribe is the best, and to make it better, we throw our messes over the fence for neighbouring tribes to deal with. They add some of their mess to it and throw it back to us. We waste a lot of time and energy cleaning up each other's messes.

I am a technology executive with years of experience fighting the silo effect that plagues organizations of all sizes. At TD Bank, where I work, we also faced this dilemma. I have learned that when we break down the barriers to communication and collaboration, we thrive as humans and as organizations.

We call our software engineering tribes "pods." Other companies call themselves "two-pizza teams" or "squads." We are all skilled at developing secure, reliable, functional software and that's what we love to do. When integrating our masterpieces with those of the other tribes, we confirm what we already know, our software is a piece of art and their software sucks. A battle develops through which we learn what drove our decisions and assumptions.

As we become familiar with each other, mutual acceptance emerges. We commit our changes, and then run through continuous integration with the other teams' dependencies, then continuous deployment and finally, continuous delivery. When ready, we let our customers use and adopt our masterpiece while we move on to something else and the cycle continues. Every time we add a new piece to the puzzle, our system expands. Our masterpieces blend, and the integrations become more complex. The battles with other tribes may become fiercer, but we always push through them so that we can go back to our happy place, developing code with our tribe.

You are probably thinking that this doesn't feel that hard to solve. After all, agile software development was invented to organically drive collaboration. Further, one of its main principles is to break a problem down into smaller pieces. But ask yourselves, are we good at stitching the solution back together? When we are developing software, do we think of it as a piece of a much larger whole? I was a software engineer for many years and happily worked in silos without even being aware of it.

I will share my favourite story of how we broke silos by intentionally driving collaboration, and how this transformation has made us more resilient. My aim is to offer these insights so that they may help other teams thrive.

What Did the Transformation Look Like?

In the Spring of 2016, after a stint in Tech Risk and Infosec, close to wrapping up my MBA, I was excited to go back to software development and interested in how digital could help shape the future of the sector. TD was well underway in its digital transformation and agile journeys and I was energized when I joined the digital team.

The specific tribe that I was now a part of was two years into replacing a 20-year-old web-based monolith with a restful architecture supported with Angular UI. The new Beta version went live, and about 90% of our active customers had started using it. We were flying! And, that was a good and important thing because our tribe had something to prove. In the fall of 2014, a yearly ranking by a major Canadian newspaper gave us an average rating, and said that we were stuck in the '90s.

Following this report, we put a lot of effort into the transformation of our platform and we were one of TD's first agile factories to get it right. We talked about the customer all the time. Our tech team didn't write a line of code without thinking of the impact on our users. To improve our customers' experience, we regularly conducted surveys and incorporated sprint retrospectives and feedback sessions. We continuously pushed out improvements in small increments. We also struck the right balance between the product and the platform. This was the basis of the strong collaboration within our tribe. It made a lot of sense to me, and in a matter of days, I felt I belonged to this tribe.

After the introduction of the new platform, we began to encounter some bumps. There were quite a few users logging into the legacy platform and we were spending a lot of energy supporting it, instead of fully focusing on improving the new platform. It turned out that many users still preferred the old, familiar, stable, and clunky interface over the shiny star we were so proud of. Transition to the new interface generated many questions such as "where the heck did they move my button?!" On the infrastructure side, the interaction between the new front-end platform, which was installed on TD's cloud, and the downstream components, which continued to sit on the physical boxes, required some optimization. Furthermore, the downstream services were mostly shared and managed by different teams, and coordinating the changes was challenging. All of this ended up lowering our customer experience index.

What Went Wrong?

This is the point in time when I joined the team. Being new, I was less attached to this platform, which had taken the team two years to build.

SILO #1: OUR TRIBE IS ISOLATED FROM THE OTHER TD TECH TRIBES

We were the first big app on TD's internal cloud. In fact, our cloud engineering team stepped up and accelerated to operationalize it in time for our Beta Release. While we felt confident in the technology we had implemented, for any issue that was uncovered through our Beta testing, our first reaction was to blame the downstream teams for not aligning their services to our requirements. I heard my team repeatedly say, "It's not us, it's them."

So how did I swim through this? On the first day of my new job, my new boss suggested that I get to know Bill McArthur. I had known Bill from one of my previous jobs at TD. Smarter than anyone else and a brilliant Software Engineer, Bill had assembled the best development team I had ever worked with at TD. When you saw Bill's team iterating through the agile software development, you would have thought that you were at a tech startup.

So why were we having issues? While I found Bill's team innovative and creative, I learned that some found them difficult to work with. I was also interested in learning how we were improving the platform to ensure it was resilient to the changes. I sat down with Bill and asked if he had a technical roadmap. He looked at me completely puzzled. He said he felt that our business leaders were more focused on getting the new functionality deployed for our customers than in knowing how the technology platform was being evolved. This is where my enlightenment started.

Bill had this mystery pod, who was iteratively designing the platform to support the business requirements that the feature-pods were going to be working on next. It was no surprise that our feature-pods were so efficient, their work was mostly focused on enabling user interface (UI) features, adding finishing touches of logic and finalizing integration with the underlying services that were already prepared.

SILO #2: THE CONCEPT OF RESILIENCY IS UNDERSTOOD ONLY BY THE TECH TRIBE

What Bill didn't talk about was that this pod was also technically improving the platform in a way that only they truly understood. They flew under the radar because they felt that business capabilities were more valued than the technical ones.

While I learned that the team was very efficient in building new business capabilities, the fact that we had not talked about resiliency with our business leaders worried me.

Why did resiliency matter so much? After all, we were quick to remediate any bump we encountered. We got to know the downstream tribes better and the collaboration with them was improving. The problem was that our remediation efforts were reactive. By not being proactive, we did not understand how resilient the platform truly was.

It was June 2016, and the United Kingdom was heading into the referendum to decide whether to stay in or leave the European Union. On June 23 that year, in the event known as Brexit, most people in the U.K. voted to leave the E.U., which had the potential to create a lot of uncertainty and a negative economic impact on Europe and the rest of the world. The next day, as people started reacting to this news, a new bar was set around the globe for usage and volumes on many systems, including ours.

SILO #3: WE LIVED IN THE HAPPY PREDICTABLE WORLD, NOT THE REAL CHAOTIC WORLD

As people scrambled in the wake of Brexit, we saw our new app quickly reach its peak capacity. We had to stop all other work to maintain availability and performance. We learned that instead of building our system just for optimal conditions, we needed to build it and test it for the worst-case scenarios.

Based on these early learnings, platform resiliency became and has remained one of TD's top priorities. It also became a daily topic with my business partners. We agreed to make a transformational shift in how we operate and achieve resiliency through collaboration.

What Did We Learn?

While during the events I have described, resiliency emerged as the primary goal, we also pivoted around its critical ingredients: transparency, collaboration and the ecosystem between all teams involved in supporting the platform and our customers. Following are the summaries of the three lessons that we took away from this experience.

LESSON #1: TECHNOLOGY MUST NOT BE A BLACK BOX

While our business partners agreed that resiliency needed all-hands-on-deck and were interested in learning more about the technical aspect of the platform, they struggled with the fact that technology was a black-box to them. Bill and I suggested that like the business roadmap we had established for our agile factory, we also needed to establish a roadmap of technology improvements that Bill's platform pod had in plan. This is what Bill and I called the 'technology roadmap'. We further agreed to establish regular reviews, sequencing and prioritization sessions, to gradually improve the transparency of the technical work.

LESSON #2: COLLABORATION NEEDS TO BE INTENTIONAL

One day while Bill and I were chatting about our progress and what we could improve, he said: "Collaboration is hard! This agile factory doesn't just happen, I have to work very hard to make people collaborate. In a blink, they go back to working in isolation, making bad assumptions that lead to bad technical decisions and bad outcomes for our customers. I am fighting isolation every day." This was a lightbulb moment for me. While I knew that I was at my best when I let my ideas grow into something tangible through collaboration, I now also realized that we needed to intentionally drive collaboration across teams.

LESSON #3: IT'S MORE THAN AN APPLICATION — IT'S AN ECOSYSTEM

Our application relies upon several downstream TD and vendor services. As I mentioned earlier, we performed well in a predictable state, but the world we lived in was chaotic. In one example, a reliable vendor that calculated some data for one of our main screens had a capacity issue causing a performance degradation. This revealed a need to improve the resiliency of the entire platform, not just the application.

It was very interesting to learn how intertwined the team and platform resiliency was, and that improving the overall resiliency required us to focus on people, as well as on the product that we were building. As with any idea, to see it through sustainably and at scale, we needed to implement a new operational structure. We called it the "Resiliency Playbook."

Resiliency Rules

Leadership is about rallying the team around common goals. Making the goals clear and achievable is a critical first step to success in this journey. While our ultimate goal was to improve collaboration and resiliency, we knew that both were hard to measure and that they had many layers to them. Instead, the goal we set for the team was to achieve the 99.99% availability. This meant that the application would be available and functional for our customers 99.99% of the time. We knew that the only way to get there was by focusing on collaboration and resiliency, which led us to transform how we operated.

To improve transparency, the first step was to redefine the platform to be the entire ecosystem of TD and vendor services that the application relied upon. We mapped all services and their dependencies end-to-end and analyzed how they were configured, how critical they were to the customer and how they interacted with one another. We then assessed the gaps in the ecosystem that stood in the way of achieving high availability. Finally, we printed the platform map with the highlighted resiliency scores in poster format and shared it broadly. The impact was astonishing. The poster showed up on many office walls. Whenever we discussed any of the platform components, our business leaders would first look up the map to understand what we were referring to. This way our conversations quickly moved from "Why?" (the issue was happening) to "How?" (to solve it). For the first time in my career, the technology platform my team supported was not a black box to anyone!

Now that we have established transparency, we started having meaningful conversations about the technical improvements that we wanted to make. We built a three-year roadmap of these changes and regularly reviewed, sequenced and prioritized both business and technical capabilities side by side.

Considering that we already had a mature agile operational model, we were able to efficiently drive improvements in resiliency and it wasn't long before our customers started responding positively to our efforts. This made us even more determined to keep going.

Tackling collaboration was the next focus point. We came up with the concept of "one team," and we invited all TD teams who supported the components of the ecosystem to join. We collocated with several of those teams, conducted regular "Scrum of Scrums" sessions, shared ideas, and talked about the platform as something that we were all building and supporting together. Our vendors became "partners" and we made them a part of the "one team" too. We expanded our technology roadmap across the platform ecosystem.

We also made several improvements in our DevOps practice. For example, we improved our testing dramatically by scientifically modelling it across the ecosystem. We did a lot of work to uplift the platform. This required us to work together with many partners to understand each other's needs and usage patterns. We also changed how we design systems in TD. The components that power capabilities critical to our customers were now built to have redundancy and automatic failover, while the non-critical ones were controlled by circuit-breakers. We have maintained transparency by improving and sharing internal operational dashboards using tools like Grafana. Our business partners set up screens with our dashboards in their offices — allowing them to check the health of the system at any time. Our security was also better because it was now assessed and managed at the platform level, vs the component level.

To share our learnings, we published a Resiliency Playbook, which over the next few years, got adopted by many other teams and platforms in TD.

And finally, throughout this process, there emerged a diverse and collaborative tribe. In 2018, that same major Canadian newspaper that rated us so poorly four years ago, now placed us as joint-winners and best-in-class. We were labelled as blazing a trail of fast-paced innovation — a remarkable turnaround.

The Moral of the Story

When I joined the team, they were a bunch of unique and talented rebels who under Bill's leadership, failed-forward and evolved insightfully. This is what made them innovative, and looking back, this is why I had earlier described them as the best development team I have worked with. As the team matured, we started focusing on resiliency. It was very important to do this at the right time - too soon and you kill innovation, too late and you die. Over time, we struck the right balance and built a culture that was both innovative and resilient. This was reflected in many small wins. For example, a simple idea to share the end-to-end system map evolved when our business partners started posting it on the office walls, making it a common language between our business and technology teams. Over time, this team has become a cradle for piloting new business and technology concepts in TD.

Collaboration was the key next step in maturing innovation and resiliency. The insights we have gained through collaboration with other teams, industry experts and our customers have broadened our views. This has made us better able to understand and predict the outcomes of our actions under the rule of resiliency, while understanding the importance of purposeful innovation and how to encourage it at every level.

We have traded silos for a community of creative and collaborative teams who are building the TD of the future.

About Sladjana Jovanovic

Sladjana Jovanovic leads Enterprise Payments Technology team in TD Bank. She is responsible for technology transformation of Payments Modernization globally as well as for building TD's Enterprise Payments platform by incorporating stability, agility, innovation and technical excellence. In her previous role in Digital Technology, Sladjana led the Online Channel technology teams and platforms.

Sladjana joined TD in 2003 as a developer of trading and prime brokerage systems, and has since progressed through more senior roles where she was accountable for TD Securities, Wealth and Digital technology teams and platforms. She also led Technology Risk and Information Security for TD Securites. Prior to joining TD in 2003, Sladjana started her career as a Technology Programmer Associate with Goldman Sachs in New York City. She is a University of Toronto, Computer Science graduate and in 2017 she completed her MBA at Rotman School of Management.

Being a strong proponent of equal career opportunities for everyone, Sladjana is dedicated to making TD Technology the company of choice for women and creating an environment where women can thrive. Sladjana loves spending time outdoors with her two children ages 13 and 15.

Acknowledgments

I would like to thank Bill McArthur and our WebBroker team, who taught me the importance of collaboration and platform resiliency, and Leo Salom, whose leadership has motivated me to lead creatively.

About Bill McArthur

Bill McArthur is a software engineer with more than 20 years of professional experience developing, architecting and leading development teams building everything from simple web applications to large distributed systems.

Acknowledgments

I would like to thank Sladjana Jovanovic for inviting me to help her tell our story, and Mark Miller for giving us the opportunity and forum to tell it. I would also like to thank all of those that were part of the journey that our story tells - from every developer on the team, all the way to our senior executives Jeff Martin, Salim Jivraj, Richard Wilks and Paul Clark who empowered us to be successful. Lastly, I'd like to thank my wife, who during the timeframe of our story, was as understanding and supportive as she has always been.

What Not to Do When Rolling Out DevSecOps and Other Learnings

by Jasmine James

CHAPTER 5

What Not to Do When Rolling Out DevSecOps and Other Learnings

A new company and a new direction, that's what I looked forward to in my new role as an engineer for a large home automation provider. My team had been specifically formed to implement new capabilities for the emerging home automation platform that would take the industry by storm. Although I was a new grad in Computer Science from one of Georgia's leading universities, my experience related to the new role that I was filling was minimal. During my interview, my interviewer (soon-to-be manager) focused on basic concepts versus actual experience, which paved the way toward securing the position. Thankfully, I knew that I would be receiving a full overview of the vision for the new team so that the execution could be on target with expectations.

Although this position was my first experience with DevSecOps, I had more experiences later in my career. In the latter portions of this chapter I will meld the stories together to create a narrative that captures the full essence of all DevSecOps failures. Each failure contains a lesson and improvement point that is captured at the end of the chapter.

A Foundation for DevSecOps: Tools

As the efforts were underway to automate the full test suite of regression test cases for the home automation platform, the team was also defining what tools would be used for source control, artifact repository, and continuous integration/delivery. Although there were legacy tools that could be leveraged for automation through script execution, the goal was to implement more modern tools that could be extended for years after the establishment of the automation framework, to enable the regression testing. With this goal in mind, I needed to implement, evaluate, and define some tools that would allow my team and others to implement the modern framework that they aimed for. As I went through this process (twice), some themes emerged that happened to make an acronym (AEIOU) that can be easily remembered. I've used this acronym in multiple environments for deciding whether the tool was appropriate for implementation.

A — APPLICABILITY

As soon as you recognize a need, it can be simple to search and find a tool that serves your purpose. One important question to ask yourself is, "How can this tool be applied to the current environment to achieve enterprise goals?" The selected tools for the DevSecOps environment should directly reference defined enterprise goals for Development, Security, and Operations process improvements. Ideally, the tool should contribute to the improvement of new or existing measures within the competency area.

E — ENTERPRISE READINESS

As enterprises of multiple sizes adopt tooling, the availability of infrastructure resilience and support can be an important consideration. Companies that are heavily regulated or have critical operations and processes should consider tool readiness. As tools come from many points of origin these days — open source, commercial off the shelf, and SaaS (to name a few) — companies should consider the availability and support. There will be a dependency introduced to the system based on the tools you choose.

I — INTEGRATION

If there are existing tools in the organization that can be leveraged as a part of the DevSecOps ecosystem, the points of integration must be considered carefully. Given the robust solutions that are available in the tooling landscape, the existing tool can often be replaced in part or completely by a new tool to avoid an integration contention. When new tools are integrated within an ecosystem, it is important to over-engineer the integrations in case the tool is replaced in the future.

O — OVERHEAD

As new tools are introduced into the environment, there are sure to be administration and governance implications on owning teams. When evaluating tools, map the roles and responsibilities within these two areas with the owning teams. If this is completed across the organization and all stakeholders are included, the implementation and adoption of tools will be seamless.

U — USEFULNESS

As tools for DevSecOps are evaluated, it is important to recognize if the tool can be leveraged at the time of implementation. There are many situations in which tools are brought into the ecosystem when other dependent systems were not yet available. When considering goals of a lean organization, it is important not to introduce waste into the system by bringing in the appropriate tools at the wrong time.

Whoa! Who knew that deciding what tools to utilize would be such an involved process? One of the great things about having some guidelines to evaluate tools was the ability to stack tool capabilities against each other within the many categories. This structured process ensured that all attributes were scrutinized consistently. For many of the tools, additional attributes were defined so that the common components within competing tools could be ranked. Although rigorous, this process was well worth it and resulted in a clear direction as to which tools could enable the organization the best. Having been very deeply involved in the evaluation, I was now well exposed to the capabilities of the tools that were chosen. This put me in a great position to lead the actual implementation of the tools, and with the help of my team, start to drive adoption for new development activities.

During this evaluation process, the first failure occurred...

Lesson #1: Security? Where's Security?!

As the DevOps tools were evaluated and implemented, one important miss was the consideration of integration into currently existing Security Tools for SAST, DAST, and other levels of scanning. The "Integration" portion of the acronym above was considered for DevOps, but did not span to Security; thus, important integration to widely used enterprise tools were missed. Although this was indeed a failure, the tools that were used had very well documented integration for our security solutions. It's important to consider the holistic DevSecOps ecosystem when selecting new tooling.

BRING EVERYONE TO THE TABLE EARLY IN THE PROCESS

In our case, security should have been a part of defining the current tooling landscape. As the capabilities of our legacy build and deployment tools were considered, the capabilities of our security tools should have been considered as well. To facilitate this, I would recommend that you include security early and often in conversations around DevOps tooling. Approach the evaluation process from a DevSecOps perspective initially to prevent rework later in the process. Although we were not ahead of the curve in this regard, we did gather inputs from involved teams after the gap was discovered.

Lesson #2: But ... Who's Going to Own It?

After considering the type of tools we would need to enable faster delivery of software, we realized that there were some overlaps in ownership across the tools, especially when it came to security. Specifically for dependency scanning and management it was clear that there would have to be some sharing of responsibilities among teams. One of the main areas of overlap was the administration and governance function. They would need to effectively manage the continued adoption and maintenance of the tool that spanned between Dev and Sec. The first challenge, this would be a newly formed relationship for the organization. One team would be responsible for the administration of the tool and the other team would be responsible for the governance. The second challenge was that both teams were already overloaded with responsibilities. Managing a new way of working was yet another function for already busy teams.

INVEST IN THE PEOPLE TO ADMINISTER AND GOVERN THE TOOLING THAT IS IMPLEMENTED

There is a very good chance that any forecasting on the amount of involvement that will be needed from DevSecOps will be off target, it was for us. For this reason, it is very important to remain flexible as tools are being implemented and during the early stages of adoption. The worst thing to do during this stage is to fall behind on establishing policies and standards and continue to drive adoption. One example of this exact situation, in my experience, was that organization was the lack of version strategy and retention policies within the new tooling lifecycle. Although the legacy processes had a clear strategy for retention and deprecation of versions, as newer tools were implemented, establishing this same process could not be easily done. Due to the lack of functionality to easily automate processes not being present on the newer tools, this capability was not available for end users to adopt. This latter point meant that a process needed to be established, which, of course, meant time and people.

In order to ensure that policies and standards were being established as a part of the roll out of DevSecOps, we established a cadence with the individual teams to share information and considerations that should be included in the other areas.

Lesson #3: Documentation . . . That'll Do the Trick!

So we had the policies and standards, how do we now create a not so daunting path towards adoption for people within the organization that had varying levels of engagement with new tools and the DevSecOps concept in general? Initially, we focused on what most enterprises do, great documentation and processes to measure adoption. The documentation we leveraged was mostly vendor based. Unfortunately, this did not reflect our chosen implementation of the tools or our specific practice and standards that we had worked so hard to establish.

ESTABLISH EDUCATIONAL PATHWAYS TO BE LEVERAGED DURING ADOPTION

If you're reading this, you're likely thinking about starting or you are in the midst of a transformation. As you introduce new capabilities, tools, and ways of working, multiple levels of education must be introduced so that adoption is completed in the right manner. No matter what your environment looks like in the beginning of transformation, there should be a path for individuals in your organization to get to know the newly defined world. This path should directly correlate to the enterprise goals of the transformation, and ideally will provide some tangible value once taken. There are many risks to not establishing a path for people to utilize tools and methods to reach enterprise transformation goals, like:

» Enterprise Transformation goals are not met.

» Anti-Patterns are adopted and introduce additional risk to the environment.

Most enterprise organizations have a method to facilitate dissemination of information across the organization. When rolling out new concepts and ideas, leverage what is already in place. One of the largest benefits of using systems that are already there is the seamless delivery and consumption of information by the organization. Individuals are used to using these systems. By adding content around new standards and best practices into this system, you should be able to easily cultivate a level of understanding.

As we found during the rollout of new concepts, the standard methods for conveying information work in some cases. However, there will be concepts that are best applied through other means of learning such as experiential or immersive delivery. Some companies, including ours, have created a place for this type of learning that is known as a "Dojo."

Lesson #4: Practice Does Not Make Perfect. Only Perfect Practice Makes Perfect.

As new concepts were introduced in the organization we found that, although teams were taking these points into consideration during the initial implementation, subsequent implementations were becoming less and less in line with the standards that were put into place. For example, we had a team that participated in multiple learning opportunities and was coached on concepts within DevSecOps such as 12 factor, secure by design, and how to sustain a cross-functional DevOps. They were rockstars initially. But, as time progressed, the team shrank and grew which introduced new individuals that did not have the same level of exposure as the original team members. Because of this, the concepts that were once being applied across the development team were being left behind.

ENSURE THAT DEVELOPMENT PRACTICE IS AT THE FOREFRONT

Some great ways to enable learning and introduce concepts of continuous learning to your organization are as follows:

» **Utilize in-place learning platforms.** If your organization has an LMS platform in place, continuously update content and mandate continuous learning for key concepts that have a large impact on DevSecOps practice.

» **Prioritize immersive learning.** Ensure teams have a place to go when they seek out help that is specific to their implementation of DevSecOps. Many times conceptual learning just won't cut it and teams will need content that specifically addresses their challenges.

» **Enable self-paced learning to drive innovation (Pluralsight, Udemy).** In reality, given the wide span of stacks and technologies out there, being able to address all of the technological needs of the organization is not realistic. Empower the organization to explore on their own by making industry learning platforms available and easily accessible.

It is also very important to ensure that teams are aware when their development practice is failing. Thankfully there are many ways that this information can be shared with the team who use APIs to expose information available in each respective DevSecOps tool within your organization. Whether you choose to expose them through periodic reporting or continuously, in the form of a dashboard, the important thing is to empower the team with information.

Summary

No transformation commences without challenges. Organizations come in many sizes, shapes, and with varying levels of maturity, so it is paramount to remain flexible as you introduce any portion of DevSecOps. Being a leader in many of these efforts has taught me that, although you might think you know the answer to the problem, there is a good chance that the problem you think you see is not the *root* problem. Dig deep to truly understand the intricacies of the organization before attempting to deliver a DevSecOps solution. Even when you think you've reached a level of understanding of the people and practices within your space, continue to listen to those who will be impacted most by the change you're inciting. The people that will live in this new world, their thoughts and opinions, along with the enterprise goals to be met, matter most.

About Jasmine James

Jasmine is the leader of enterprise DevOps practice and enablement at a large airline. Her love for all things DevOps started with being automation minded in the quality engineering space. Jasmine transitioned into owning the holistic efficiencies of DevOps at her company by first establishing tools and then enabling developers through documentation and education to make their code better and safer. Her work these days is around increasing adoption of the cool groundwork that is in place and teaching individual contributors and leadership about the benefits of utilizing DevSecOps tools and best practices.

Jasmine currently lives in Atlanta, GA and loves to attend conferences and community events for all-things tech, especially around DevOps and Cloud. Sometimes she even speaks or writes articles about her journey within DevOps and her career. Want to see what she's up to? Find her on LinkedIn where she posts regularly.

Acknowledgments

A special thanks to Mark Miller and Derek Weeks from the Sonatype team for this opportunity to share. I have avoided many pitfalls as a result of reading or hearing about other's experiences, so I am happy to be able to share my own journey and learnings. A gigantic thanks also to my leader Keanen Wold for support as I contribute to multiple efforts within the DevOps community, and to my team for sharing their experiences with me. Finally — a special thanks to the proofreaders and copywriters that helped refine my story!

CHAPTER 6

Cultural Approaches to Transformations
Staying Safe and Healthy

by Marc Cluet

CHAPTER 6

Cultural Approaches to Transformations

Staying Safe and Healthy

I wrote this chapter of the book not to tell personal tales, but as a quick guide to exploring the minefield of mistakes that most cultural transformations make. Cultural transformations are not easy or fast, and under most circumstances, they can be nerve wrecking.

I have dedicated a good part of the last six years to helping organisations transform their culture and ways of working. I've done everything from a full DevOps transformation to adding SRE security assessments to a simple migration to the Cloud (with all the changes that this represents). I embrace agile, scrum, Kanban and all the things that make modern IT companies faster and stronger at their game.

During these journeys I have found all kinds of madness, mystery, trouble, and mistakes — some of the stories funnier than others. I will walk you through my approach and share some of the best stories, or at least those funnier ones (fun not guaranteed).

Expectations about what DevOps and DevSecOps are, and what they can provide, sit in a wild spectrum. Expectation handling becomes a wizardly art form, where everything is on fire, and not in a good, "look-at-that-fire-so-beautiful" way.

Transformation Expectations

Whenever you are exploring DevOps and DevSecOps, you can start to understand the situation you signed up for by just listening to some of the answers you get to your questions. Some of them will sound vaguely like these:

> » "Yeah, we are already doing it as we have Jenkins."
>
> » "I have a Palo Alto appliance connected to the cloud, we are secure."

> » "Yes, we do DevOps since we're doing Scrum."

> » "All our SRE is good because we have AWS CloudWatch for monitoring."

> » "Isn't DevOps and Cloud the same thing?"

If you haven't heard any of these, you might have a false sense of confidence. Any cultural transformation is complex; one attached to a technical transformation is even more so. Companies decide to transform for technical or market reasons, which means that not only will you have a complex technical and cultural transformation, but also a very strict timeline in which to deliver it.

HAVE NO FEAR... FOLLOW A METHOD OF DISCOVERY

So first of all, don't panic! We have all been in situations like this. Alcoholism is still an option (not a great one), but before we start drinking, let's try taking a constructive approach.

The first thing to understand is what the company really expects out of the transformation. Companies are driven by people, and sometimes people make decisions with little information at hand. It reminds me of when I purchased my first car — I thought I was making the right decision but I realise now that I didn't know much, and the choice I made was more from a gut instinct than anything else.

In order to help them buy a better car, it's important to understand the pain they are experiencing. Is it market pressure? Money bleeding? Not having anyone in IT who is good at Cobol? It's your task to find out, and while you are doing it remember: avoid judgement. We all have awkward moments we don't speak of, and you will be going through their awkward moments.

Once we have an initial idea of the situation and what the real problems are, remember that DevOps is all about People, Culture, and Tools — in that order. You need to categorise problems and understand how they correlate and interact.

SET THE RIGHT EXPECTATIONS

Engineering is hard, culture is harder! Be conservative about expectations, present a full picture, and be realistic about the difficulty of the mission. Create very clear checkpoints and schedule stop/go decision meetings.

Prepare a transformation roadmap, and as with any roadmap, make sure that objectives are well defined in the near horizon, with broader and more generic objectives defined as you move further forward in time.

Keep communications frequent, and ensure a proper feedback loop so the plan can be adapted as events develop.

FAIL EARLY, LEARN QUICKLY

There is a lot to write about cultural and technical transformations, and all of it cannot be covered in this chapter. My recommendation is to learn and adapt. If you are unsure about anything, do a small, time-contained experiment, validate, and move forward. Learn as quickly as possible from anything that goes wrong.

Where Things Can Go Wrong

Hey that's why you have this book! To learn from other people's mistakes! I have been around long enough to see a ton of them. Some of them I was able to help fix, while others I wanted to fix and couldn't. Here are some of the lessons I learned.

TRANSFORMATION BY COMMITTEE SLOWS THINGS DOWN

Any transformation is bound to make someone sad, or mad, or both — it is part of any change.

I've found myself in several projects where every single step of transformation was not only decidedly risk-averse, but also had decisions made by a huge committee, where every single part of the company had a voice. I've even found myself in projects with weekly tracking and decision-making sessions for next steps.

Decision paralysis by committees often kills momentum. The number of issues that bounce back to the committee, along with the cadence of the committee meetings themselves, end up defining the speed of decision making.

DON'T FEAR COMMITMENT

In big established companies one of the most valuable assets is people. People create the company's core values and help through good and bad times. Unfortunately, cultural transformations, even partial ones, do change the paradigm and challenge conventions inside a company. This inevitably creates tension inside the business, as we humans are generally not great dealing with change and tend to find a stable environment more comfortable.

Leadership can, and sometimes will, use this as an excuse to not commit to any change, in fear of losing people. The inherent question then is how to move forward with enough motivation.

Conquistador Hernán Cortés, as he arrived in America, made sure everyone understood that there was no way back by breaking his ships (some people say he burned them, others say that he just made them incapable of sailing). You need someone in Leadership to metaphorically burn those ships, and decisively show the way forward. This can be done by someone already in a leadership role or by bringing in someone new.

RISK-AVERSE BUSINESSES CAN'T ADAPT

There are some businesses that are rightly built around risk aversion. This is especially true for insurance and banks — we would not put our money in a bank that would leak data or lose our transfers, would we? At the same time, the sector is under severe pressure to modernise itself. It has done so successfully in the past, but this time the stakes are higher. There is mounting competition from FinTech and other startups with no legacy, ready to take on the market, and they are capable of adapting more quickly to not only the market's needs but also to regulatory frameworks.

While transforming businesses within this footprint is the most challenging, it can also be the most rewarding. It is especially important to do isolated experimentation, validate the model and expand, avoid decisions by committee as much as possible, and reach agreement from leadership to help push the envelope.

AVOID SOFTWARE ARCHITECTURE MISMATCHES

Writing software nowadays is a different experience from what it was when big projects using ITIL and waterfall were the norm. Now, due to the increased need to go to the market quickly, gathering feedback and iterating the product design often gets us to the desired state better than doing one, big-bang release.

There is an inherent danger with trying to adapt to this new way of writing antifragile, microservice-based software. By doing things too quickly or by using a team that only knows how to write monolithic software, you can end up in a position where a team has created a "microservice monolith" with such strong couplings that you lose most of the advantages of separating functionality in smaller bits of software.

Education about this is especially important, as greenfielding and chiselling the monolith away will be a crucial part of any transformation.

CENTRALISATION VS. DECENTRALISATION IS A DIFFICULT DECISION

I have experienced excruciating amounts of pain especially on the subject of finding the right balance of engineering liberty vs. centralisation of engineering processes (and tooling).

Neither end of the spectrum is beneficial for the long-term flexibility and happiness of the engineering team. I've seen companies struggle heavily with this. It is a problem that if not resolved properly can bring severe, long-term pain. It's like trying to go on an extreme fattening diet or an extreme weight-loss diet: neither will be good for you.

If you give complete liberty to the engineering teams, they will come up with several different ways of solving the same problem. It is creativity at its finest and best, but at the same time, if you plan to carry forward every single different method, it will likely have to be supported and maintained by someone with a less positive view of the world.

AVOID "NOT-BUILT-HERE" SYNDROME

Whenever a new culture emerges, there is a pressing need to have new tooling to be able to enable this new way of working. There is also a temptation to write the whole thing in-house, in order to craft exactly to the needs of the business, like some kind of very patient Swiss watchmaker performing their Opus Magnus.

This will normally lead to a situation where, while there is initially all kinds of investment and excitement about the rosy future, you end up rediscovering the large overhead of maintaining your own software — and the headaches this involves.

UNDERSTAND THE CI/CD DIVIDE

Another problem of rapid upskilling is understanding the difference between Continuous Integration (CI) and Continuous Delivery (CD) — they are very different beasts.

Continuous Integration is the most well known and already covered by tooling; there are prominent tools and a big community around it.

But, a lot of companies will try to use the same hammer for Continuous Delivery even though Continuous Delivery requires a completely different set of tools. It has very different requirements around predictability and adaptability of deployment. Using CI tools for CD is a clear anti-pattern that needs to be eradicated, just like broad trousers of the nineties.

Some Ideas on How to Reach Success

This is by no means a bible or a step-by-step guide, but here are some ideas I'm throwing in your general direction and hope will inspire you.

KNOW THE PAIN THRESHOLD

We all have a certain amount of tolerance for pain (or liking of, if you're into that, no judgement). Companies and groups have their own tolerance as well, so it's important to understand which things you are allowed to stretch, play with and challenge, and which ones are part of the core belief of the group. There is no transformation, either cultural or technical, that will not go through a certain amount of pain, so make sure everyone understands and accepts this and declares the "no-go" zones that they feel can irreversibly damage the culture of the company.

BALANCE TEAM ORG VS. OUTCOME

Conway's Law states that "organizations which design systems ... are constrained to produce designs which are copies of the communication structures of these organizations." This is painfully true. Creating new team topologies without transforming the current ones can also create problems its.

Rearranging teams in a way that matches your desired end state will reduce efficiency and velocity on the short term, but it will accelerate the adoption of new methodologies, which in the long term will pay back tenfold.

APPLY THE "RUBBER BANDS THEORY"

All cultural and technical transformations will create tension. If we look at DevOps in general we can all agree that it's all about People, Process, and Tools (strictly in that order).

If we push change too quickly on people, the processes might suffer when they're not ready for that new pace. There's no advantage to changing tools too quickly, without reviewing processes or upskilling people.

The rubber band theory (which I coined, no trademark, use away!) likens People, Process, and Tools to levers which are connected by rubber bands. By pushing one lever and not the others, you create tension on the other two which can become too much and snap the rubber band. We must aspire to move all three levers at the same pace to keep tension to a minimum.

ADOPT ZERO TRUST, AND SHIFT LEFT

Security nowadays is still considered an afterthought — some heavy-plated armour to add to the structure after it has been built, then connected with thin wires and roughly finished.

Cloud computing and any kind of public computing should always be considered a zero-trust zone. Security should always be involved from the beginning, even if you're having initial thoughts about an idea in the shower (well, maybe not there...). They should always be there, helping, collaborating, and ensuring that the application is coded defensively with security in mind. Don't wait until the last minute to add security — that will be too late.

APPLY THE BLACKBOX THEORY

When you have lots of microservices they naturally get handed over to teams who grow them and do whatever is needed to deliver high-quality software. Reaching an agreement on handover between domains of influence is always a prickly task, as tension is more predominant at the boundaries themselves.

If you give full control and liberty to the teams, some of the economy of repetition and automation can be lost. At the same time, not giving enough liberty will limit the innovation and speed of delivery, which is about as great as driving an amazing car in bumper-to-bumper traffic.

One solution I normally suggest is to adopt the blackbox theory, which creates domain-exclusive zones — but, all the boundary zones need to be agreed on across the organization. One of the ways this manifests is an approach of "APIs everywhere," in which all applications expose their functionality as API calls. Blackbox theory can also be applied to monitoring and other areas where there is a predominant advantage of having a common framework to ensure correlation of all the data and a smooth end-to-end journey, as microservices can definitely make the approach be seen as inconsistent if the teams are too loosely bound. This can be a design decision, as AWS does with their services.

MAINTAIN CLEAR DIFFERENTIATION BETWEEN CI AND CD

Continuous Integration and Continuous Delivery have completely different requirements, and keeping a very clear separation barrier is not only important, but essential. I normally even encourage using different software for one and the other; CI and CD should not touch or coexist in the same Jenkins pipelines. Continuous Delivery will require things like automatic rollback, blue/green deployment, automatic load balancing, version validation, and smoke testing through the release. None of those can be provided by run-of-the-mill CI software.

Real Life Scenarios (Yes, it Happened)

Alright, I kind of lied. Earlier, I alluded that I would not tell you about incidents I was personally involved in, but here are some real-world examples. I won't mention company names and all personal details have been changed.

SCENARIO 1: THE COMPANY THAT WANTED TO CLOUD

I was approached by a company that wanted to move all their services from several data centres across the UK into a full Cloud approach — they wanted a dual Cloud strategy approach and this was one of the requirements from the beginning.

As I was starting to interview different teams and understand the real desire behind the transformation itself, there was a game being played between some of the leadership in this company and account managers from (quite big) Cloud providers. The result of that was that the whole strategy of Cloud migration would change almost on a daily basis, depending on who made a more compelling offer for their services.

This company had a Cloud transformation committee that was meeting weekly, and it would make good recommendations, but Leadership would ignore them most of the time, until eventually the committee was disbanded.

Understanding these were signs of a transformation that was doomed, I encouraged the company to take control of the transformation and build their own team, which they ended up doing. This is in itself an anti-pattern (if you read Team Topologies it is clear), but it was a short-lived step towards ensuring that there was a single head responsible, as this would help encourage the right conversations and avoid all the infighting about how to do things without clear lines of accountability.

This one was a real roller coaster — a short, intense one!

SCENARIO 2: GROWING PAINS OF SUCCESS

There is this web company that did all the right things: they had microservices and teams that had clear responsibility over microservices. The problem they needed to solve was that the teams had so much liberty that they ended up creating their own full ecosystems — from deployment to monitoring, and the kitchen sink. This created a lot of overhead and the quickly growing company found itself in a position where it was impossible to track a customer journey across several services. It also spent not-insignificant amounts of money on the overhead of having to maintain ten different ways of doing the same thing, all of which were handed back to a central Platform Engineering team which could suggest approach but had no final say.

We had to take a more radically direct approach to this, first going through all the teams and understanding their pain, their issues, and what motivated and drove them. This took the best part of three months.

Once this initial phase was finished, we came up with a boundary framework, something that could be used to define inputs and outputs for all the different services. This would help have a centralised monitoring and security stream and allow a full view of the system. We also encouraged centralising some of the deliverables that were not central to the team "raison d'etre" like how to spin up containers, maintain a container repository, or security scan new components.

In Conclusion

Transformation is a very hard business — if it was easy it would not have fostered a whole industry of its own. There is a lot to read out there, and a lot to learn from going through the pains of driving a transformation yourself. Remember to set the right expectations and take a proper investigative approach — usually people understand the problems but that does not mean they fully understand the underlying issues. Make sure you have the right support from Leadership and stakeholders.

Be very aware where things can go wrong, as you will have to correct things quickly and smoothly. And always try to accomplish a successful transformation with open communication, setting the right expectations and timelines.

I hope to have inspired you enough to have a try at this — it is certainly more challenging than Engineering, at least for me! Safe journey.

About Marc Cluet

Marc Cluet is the Founder at Ukon Cherry, a London-based consultancy specialising in DevOps, and has over 22 years of experience in the Industry, including with companies like Rackspace, Canonical, Trainline, DevOpsGroup, Nationwide Building Society, plus several startups across five different countries. Marc has also spoken in some of the most prestigious conferences including FOSDEM, LISA, OpenStack Summit, UDS, Puppetconf, and several meetups. Marc is one of the organisers of London DevOps which is the second biggest DevOps meetup in the world, and he helps organise DevOps Exchange Barcelona and Barcelona Big Data.

Marc has contributed code to several projects including Puppet, mcollective, Juju, and cloud-init, and helped create MAAS. He loves solving complex infrastructure problems and applying solid and repeatable solutions. He is also an expert in building up agile engineering teams.

Acknowledgments

For their inspiration and collaboration, I would like to thank Mark Miller, Derek Weeks, Matt Saunders, Jack Moore, Alex Dover, Jordi Duran, Tony Chapman, Stephen Thair, Paul Heywood, Dominique Top, Nic Ferrier, Avleen Vig, Juan Negron, Robert Collins, Michael Man, Chuck Short, Ivan Pedrazas, Chris Turvil, and Marcus Maxwell. Thanks for leading the way.

I would also like to thank the reviewers for all their amazing feedback: Alek Kras, Binyam Asfaw, Baptiste Durant-Bret and Ai V.

DEV
SEC
OPS
DAYS

The Seven Deadly Sins of DevSecOps

by Ryan Lockard

CHAPTER 7

The Seven Deadly Sins of DevSecOps

"Finally, we're seeing that nearly everyone understands security is a business risk issue at the end of the day. I joke with my clients, 'the board gets it, so they want to do something about cybersecurity, that's the good news." But the bad news is, 'the board gets it and they want to do something about cybersecurity.' But of course it really is good news."

— Bruno Haring, Director, Cybersecurity & Privacy, PwC;
President, InfraGard Atlanta, at SecureWorld Atlanta

In my consulting job with Contino, we partner with the world's largest regulated enterprises and try to help them with their cloud journey and adoption of DevOps practices. We place a strong focus on making security a major part of both the cloud and the operating culture of these organizations that partner with us. This level of access gives me a pretty unique and validated understanding of the industry's security posture. While I am not going to be discussing any of my clients (past or present) in this chapter, I will be pulling from my 20 years in the industry seeing DevSecOps applied, or more commonly misapplied.

In addition to my time as a consultant I'm also finding my early years in school very relevant in understanding the perils and pitfalls of DevSecOps transformations. For the first 12 years of my schooling, my mother thought I would be well served to attend catholic school — be it a desire to temper my youthful exuberance, apply structure to my otherwise free spirited ways or perhaps, just to fulfill the obligations of her Irish-Catholic upbringing. The theory was that being educated in a structure that is steeped in dogma and doctrine would imbibe similar structure to me. So, I came up in the Philadelphia Catholic School system, which is ironic, as I write this today as a non-practicing, non-denominational person.

As much as I no longer follow the dogma, a lot of the teaching is still very much part of who I am.

It is said in Roman Catholicism that each of the seven deadly sins is uniquely bad. Any time one of these sins are committed, we must confess them and do all that we can to not transgress again. Applying the DevSecOps context, each of the failures discussed in this chapter are an opportunity to reflect, inspect and improve our own DevSecOps practices every day.

Pride

Change is hard. In my everyday conversations as a DevOps consultant, I speak to many organizations and leaders across the globe. Some of these are customers, others potential customers and some just folks asking for insights. The one common theme throughout is that the desire to change the operating model and technical posture of the organization is not nearly strong enough to overcome the forces that resist the change.

Given my principal focus on the highly regulated enterprise, I tend to encounter a large number of organizations that have already attempted one, two, ten, DevOps or Cloud "transformations." But nearly all miss the return they are seeking. Often times managers say the teams will not learn or change enough, and the teams say the managers are not actually changing the structure enough to allow for lasting organizational change.

One of the clearest markers for limited change I can point to comes from the 2019 Sonatype DevSecOps Community Survey. When asked how teams are informed of DevSecOps issues, the results are broken into two groups: respondents with Elite DevOps Practices and those without. Among the two groups, you see fairly similar results, with being informed from the Security Team as the most frequent, broadcast emails second, manager/boss third, and customers (really?! ffs) fourth. But the other response is where the interesting bit lies. The chasm between those teams that were informed from tooling that have elite DevOps practices (63%) and those without the DevOps practices (39%) is significant.

Now, does that mean there is limited or no security scanning tooling in those not being informed by the tools? I would wager a guess not. Having spent 17 years in highly regulated enterprises myself, before moving to consulting, I have seen first hand (and have the scars to prove it) that tooling is not the issue here.

But automated tooling can cause problems if it does not clearly support the goals of the organization, or the mindset required to configure or interpret the tooling outputs is lacking such that the tools are rendered useless. One blatant example was a team I assumed leadership over that had a security scan that emailed you every 30 minutes if there were no issues found. Read that last sentence again. Right, you're back now. So if there was a security issue, you would *not* get the email. This pattern literally created a noise channel. Within a week of being there I was added to the alert emails, and in under an hour questions were asked. It took some time for me to find someone that could intelligently talk about the use of this alert since most had created an email filter to stave off the annoyance.

This point is further validated in another finding from the Sonatype report:

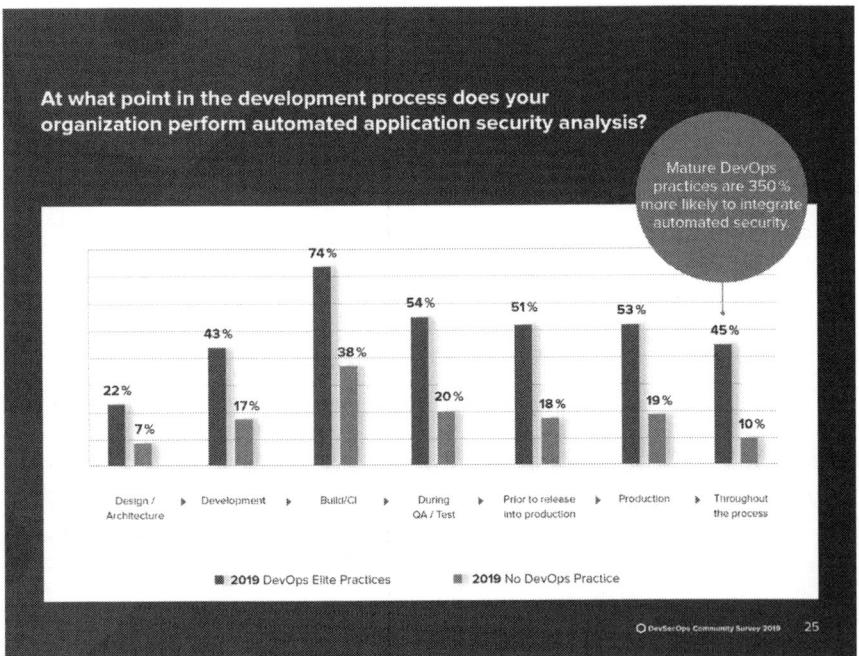

At what point in the development process does your organization perform automated application security analysis?

Mature DevOps practices are 350% more likely to integrate automated security.

	Design / Architecture	Development	Build/CI	During QA / Test	Prior to release into production	Production	Throughout the process
2019 DevOps Elite Practices	22%	43%	74%	54%	51%	53%	45%
2019 No DevOps Practice	7%	17%	38%	20%	18%	19%	10%

■ 2019 DevOps Elite Practices   ■ 2019 No DevOps Practice

DevSecOps Community Survey 2019   25

Too often, non-enlightened organizations are implementing a tool or tooling solution without appreciating the intent of the tool, educating the internal customer of the tooling signal, or applying simple telemetry and dash boarding around tooling signals such as SLIs (Service Level Indicators) and SLOs (Service Level Objectives). Said differently, too often traditional organizations are not embracing security culture and security education for teams in a meaningful way. This is genuinely one of the largest areas of damage in the enterprise today. Too few people really understand the complexity of cloud computing, distributed systems, event driven architectures, containers, functions, microservices, etc, let alone how to secure these technologies one step faster than the bad actors. What's worse, too many are too prideful to even admit they need help.

Greed

Have you ever seen "Hoarders?" It's a reality TV show that dives into the story of a person that exhibits the attributes of the compulsive hoarding mental illness. They deep dive into the life of someone who has packed their house with a lifetime of collections, newspapers, jars, dolls, or whatever else they have come across. It's a portrait of the imprisonment of the afflicted person. Despite a strong desire to break the cycle, they can't do it without outside help. The show then attempts to help by bringing in loved ones and professionals to course correct the disorder. Usually with happy results.

Most teams I have worked with in my career are brownfield teams. The software code they work in is usually older than five years. It is the aggregation of multiple languages and a hodgepodge of libraries — open, closed and custom sourced. Too many times, these monolithic systems have little to no automated unit or functional tests. Sometimes there will be superficial security scans, but pretty poor by modern standards. These are code hoarders. Admittedly, the teams themselves are not greedy. They did not desire to have this much debt. By several means (often organizations that value output over outcomes or devaluation of SOLID principles) these systems have been created by a nameless cadre that likely have never written code in their life, nor do they express empathy for the danger of working in such a codebase. I affix the greed to that group.

48%, or nearly half, of the non-elite DevOps organizations have no standards for how open source or third-party libraries are used in their ecosystems. Given there are no standards, it is not a massive leap to assume they have no f*&#ing clue which libraries are even in the codebase. In the Wrath section, the concept of the

Software Bill of Materials is further discussed, but this concept is a massive security vector that should be applied in these regressive organizations.

With this degree of code sprawl, we should look at the cost of security breaches to quantify the risk in such code bases. Globally, the average cost per security breach in 2019 was $3.92M. That cost balloons to $8.19M if you live in the United States. In 2019 it took an average of 279 days for a security breach to be discovered by the impacted organization. With a delay like that, it is interesting to understand how the cost of that breach hits the organizations financials. As you'd expect, the largest impact is felt in the first year, 67%. In the second year, 22% of the financial impact of the security breach hits the company's books, and then there is an additional 11% that lingers for years three and longer.

If you are familiar with American Baseball, you may recognize why I call this the Bobby Bonilla contract of DevSecOps. But the New York Mets only signed that contract once (they signed the infamous contract in 2001 and it pays $1.5M per year till 2035). Unfortunately for us, this is a recurring cost for each and every security breach that is realized. If you are involved in security, data, release management, product management or any number of other areas and intend to continue to be gainfully employed, it is imperative to stop being greedy with your code, and start building a mindful security roadmap.

Lust

Who doesn't have a plan for utilizing Kubernetes yet? Anyone?

Unless you've been living under a rock for the last two years you know that Kubernetes has been garnering a lot of attention in the technology space. Kubernetes is an open-source container-orchestration system for automating application deployment, scaling, and management. It was originally designed by Google, and is now maintained by the Cloud Native Computing Foundation. It aims to provide a "platform for automating deployment, scaling, and operations of application containers across clusters of hosts."

I remember hearing my colleague, Robert Geisheimmer, giving a talk in 2019 in Chicago. His topic was around Kubernetes, and he started by asking who in the room was running Kubernetes. About 20 of the folks in the room acknowledged they were. He asked something along the lines of "Who here is running Kubes

native?" — meaning Kubernetes deployed by hand, rather than as a managed service. In a room of about 50 people, from all sorts of companies in the Chicagoland
area, 10 hands went up — so 50% of the folks in the room were running
Kubernetes the hard way. Rob then made a very poignant comparison. He asked a
seemingly detached question: "Who here drives a car." As you might assume with
an American audience, nearly every single hand went up. He then asked, "How
many of you have built your car from the engine, to the frame, to the doors roof
and windows?" Not a single hand went up. Rob also showed 13 lines of code he
had prepared to stand up a fully functioning Kubernetes cluster in Google Cloud,
on GKE. He also deployed a simple containerized application from this code. His
point was simple. You do not always have to do things the hardest way possible.
Engineers (software or security) oftentimes seek the novel (colorful) solution,
when the simpler solutions are sometimes better.

Nearly all of my customers desire to run applications on Kubernetes. Be it EKS,
GKE, AKS, PKS, OpenShift or Native, there is a core belief that Kubernetes is the
magic pill for all that ails the enterprise. I recently spoke to a very senior potential
customer who fundamentally believed that Kubernetes was a required vehicle to
get to the cloud. Kubernetes, like the wonders of pre-assembled cars, is a wonder-
ful advancement. It allows for distributed computing at speed and scale, the likes
of which we have not known in human history. It also presents a plethora of security considerations (exponentially more so when run natively) than ever before. If
you struggled to maintain security with non-Kubernetes workloads, what makes
you confident you will do better with them? Hope?

In a Kubernetes system, the operators must be aware of dozens of either unique
or advanced concepts such as Role Based Access Controls (RBAC), cluster-wide
pod security policies, namespace established security boundaries, encryption of
secrets at rest, container scanning, honeypot containers, short lived containers,
etc. The list is immense. When we offload some of the responsibility to the public
cloud providers, by leveraging a vendor Kubernetes service, such as Amazon
Web Services EKS service, we start to enjoy some security and cognitive relief.
In simple terms we no longer have to worry about the security *of the cloud*, we
just have to concern ourselves with the security on the cloud. For example, AWS
shoulders the security responsibility of EKS as it relates to the control plane nodes
and etcd database. This is audited by outside firms to assure the highest level of
compliance. The EKS customer is still responsible for the securing of data plane,
security groups, scanning of containers (and the containers themselves), and other
elements, but a large collection of the core security is offloaded.

Gluttony

Working in the federal space seems exceptionally difficult. I have gotten close, working on a Federal Information Security Management Act (FISMA) compliant project once or twice in my career, but for the most part have tactically missed out on working for long periods in the federal space. I like to think that those who do work in the federal space have our federal systems secure and locked down, but as we have learned through the public record of what has happened with Edward Snowden and Wikileaks, even the most hardened systems are vulnerable. But what is unique about the U.S. government is that FISMA requires the Office of Management and Budget (OMB) to report annually their findings of incidents around cybersecurity.

Below is part of the executive summary of the 2017 OMB report:

> Although this progress is encouraging, agencies endured 35,277 cybersecurity incidents in Fiscal Year (FY) 2017, which is a 14% increase over the 30,899 incidents that agencies reported in FY 2016, with five of the FY 2017 incidents reaching the threshold of "major incident" due to their impact. OMB, DHS, and agency partners must continue to act to reduce the disruption that cybersecurity incidents have on the Federal enterprise. Accordingly, this annual FISMA report to Congress highlights government-wide programs and initiatives as well as agencies' progress to enhance Federal cybersecurity over the past year and into the future.

Let's break this down a little. At the meta layer, it's natural to think the U.S. government will face cybersecurity attacks. Every black hat, from nuisance to bad actor likely sees the U.S. government system as its white whale, and for some reason decides to occasionally throw a harpoon at that whale. But what is interesting here is the increase in incidents. As a cynic, I am quick to assume the bureaucracy of the federal government is likely not allowing for real-time threat detection, vulnerability remediation or artificial intelligence to derive typical patterns so that one can detect atypical patterns around access or data query. And sadly, my black cynical heart is proven right. Let's deconstruct the five "major" incidents (all disclosed in the public report):

INCIDENT 1 — DEPARTMENT OF HOMELAND SECURITY

With the word "Security" in its title, how bad can this major incident actually be? Let's look at the report itself:

"On May 11, 2017, the Acting CISO of DHS's Office of the Inspector General (OIG) reported to DHS officials that the sensitive personal information of 246,167 DHS employees had been discovered on the home computer of a DHS employee. An additional 159,000 case files from the OIG's investigative case management system were also found."

Say what? OK, but how critical could that data be? I mean, let's not get ahead of ourselves. This could be data like an employee's start date that is less critical. But no, the data that was compromised contained the names, Social Security numbers, dates of birth, positions, grades, and duty station data for the ~250K federal employees. In layman's terms, someone walked out of a secure, federal building with a quarter million people's most valuable PII (personally identifiable information) on (presumably) a thumb drive, and it set off no alerts. According to the DHS, they will be doing better. They are going to implement more security and data access controls as well as look at usage patterns of those with access.

INCIDENT 2 — DEPARTMENT OF TREASURY

Looking at the report: "On March 3, 2017, IRS identified a breach in which 100,210 taxpayers had their Adjusted Gross Income information exposed to unauthorized parties via impersonation through its Data Retrieval Tool."

This data-retrieval tool was largely used for the application for federal student aid. The compromise started in 2016. A group of hackers found the exposed data and used it to manipulate the student aid system. They were able to file upwards of 8,000 applications and fraudulently collect up to $30M in student aid money. There were no automated systems in place to detect the fraud, there were no data or endpoint scans in place to identify the open access and there were not even manual checks in place to validate the funds were distributed to legitimate people. This type of failure is of critical importance because it shows how asleep one can be at the wheel. Even with the (sometimes) security theater of compliance such as FISMA High, it is still possible to architect and release systems that expose PII that can be acted upon to steal taxpayer money.

INCIDENT 3 — DEPARTMENT OF TRANSPORTATION

"On November 1, 2016, DOT identified and notified US-CERT, OMB, and Congress of an inadvertent disclosure on one of its public-facing websites. DOT determined that the breach was not a result of malicious intent or compromise."

INCIDENT 4 — FEDERAL ENERGY REGULATORY COMMISSION

"A malicious actor attempted to compromise Commission employees' email accounts. As a result, email for six users was forwarded to an unauthorized source."

INCIDENT 5 — OFFICE OF THE COMPTROLLER OF THE CURRENCY (OCC)

"Prior to retirement, a former OCC employee downloaded more than 10,000 encrypted files that included Controlled Unclassified Information (CUI) and PII to two removable thumb drives."

While the United States government has access to a high amount of tax-payer backed funding, they seem to overlook the most basic of security patterns available. There is an appearance to feast upon the learned behavior and operating models of the past. This feasting has bred complacency, and from the complacency has emerged issues. Thankfully, there is a recent ray of hope. As of the 2020 National Defense Authorization Act (2020 NDAA), there is now a requirement within the Secretary of Defense to establish the use of Agile DevOps development practices as an alternative for the joint strike fighter autonomic logistic information system.

So, while the gluttony of the past typically predicts the gluttony of the future, it is refreshing to see a bill passed that requires the federal eye be gazed upon more modern security approaches.

Wrath

May 2017 I was working for a larger enterprise in downtown Philadelphia and I was running my own development team for a much larger line of business. As is the case with large corporations, we all directly reported to a Senior Vice President (SVP) who worked for the Chief Information Officer. This organization did not have a CTO, so the SVP was effectively the CTO. I had worked for him for about four years at this point, and we had a "trust but verify" relationship, it was bi-directional.

My team was operating a compliant platform that is used in a clinical setting in the United States. We had also migrated this entire platform to the cloud a few years earlier. We leaned on the shared responsibility model of the cloud as well as the well documented case studies on how to maintain HIPAA compliance with distributed cloud workloads. It sounds complex and interesting, but it really wasn't. At the time, we were meeting our revenue and growth numbers for the product. I was also working tightly with this team on improving the people and process side of the department. We focused a lot on our branching and merging hygiene, we made pair/mob-programming a first class practice, we also were using Octopus Deploy for a few years as our Continuous Integration tooling since we were a .Net team. Obviously we had dependencies on various libraries and Open Source tools that were outside of .Net, but that was our core. We had millions of lines of .Net in our platform.

The team went from one of the worst performing groups in the organization to a pinnacle of engineering both from a resiliency and from a developer experience perspective. The SVP himself even noted to me a few times how impressed he was with how this team had rounded out over the years.

On this particular morning, I saw that SVP frantic. I'd seen it before. While he was typically mild mannered and much more reserved than the typical person, he would have his dynamic moments. He was bolting across the 18th floor. I hadn't even reached my desk, I was still wearing my jacket and backpack. When he was like this, I knew it was best to avoid him. In spite of my best efforts, there was a momentary locking of the eyes, and he made a bee line for me. He looked at me and said, "Oh thank god, your team is a .Net team. You are fine...." My curiosity now piqued, I asked what he was talking about. At that moment, he was the first to tell me about the yet-to-be-named attack now known as WannaCry. After getting him to slow down a little, I asked a little more detail. I got the five-cent tour of an executive's understanding of a ransomware attack that he had just been briefed on 30 minutes prior. Neither his explanation nor his assertion that we were fine because we were a ".Net shop" resonated with me. To make matters worse, I then was told "Oh, you're also in the cloud. You are fine." At that point, I knew I had to scrap my morning plans and really unpack whatever the hell was really going on. After 5-7 minutes of Googling I knew I was not, as he said, *fine*.

Over the course of my time with that team, I had done a few smart things — I also have my share of bonehead moves there too. One of those smart things was to hire a couple of really, really smart people. One of those people made an effort to start an inventory of all of the software we had running on our systems. Today, I know this is called the Software Bill of Materials (SBOM) a practice, but at the time we just called it the "inventory." I pulled together a SWAT team to assess which items in the inventory would be most susceptible to the struts vulnerabilities, and which would be the next most vulnerable. We then used a set of tools to do vulnerability scans (I believe we were principally using masscan and nmap at that time). Sure enough, we found vulnerabilities. I made sure we followed procedures to remediate the very few incidents we found, and we continued to scan lesser susceptible areas.

That spring day, a few poignant lessons were inadvertently taught to me:

» You cannot patch what you do not know exists.

» Never, ever, go on word of mouth from anyone as to the security of your system. If the code doesn't say you are safe, you are not safe. Even when the code says you are good, trust but verify.

» Too few organizations and teams really know all of the software running on their systems. Today there are a few tools on the market that automate a lot of the vulnerability or automate the versioning of libraries (such as the Nexus Repository service), but the only way for these tools to be effective is by creating a security-first and zero-trust mindset in the engineering culture of the organization.

» Security is not the responsibility of a particular department, it is everyone's responsibility in the engineering group.

» Software Bill of Materials (SBOMs) are baller. If you don't have one for your project, you really should create one.

Sloth

Back in 2006, I was an ambitious, corporate, technical project manager. Five years out of school, with a job that I hoped to have within the decade, I was living the dream. I was working for a global enterprise that was fully invested in the Oracle e-Business Suite. Nearly all of my work was focused on that core ERP and associated applications. The only work I did outside of Oracle customization and maintenance was related to the management and migration of servers and data centers.

That year I was asked to lead one of the projects associated with a major upgrade of the core Oracle eBusiness Suite. We were aiming to upgrade the software from version 11.5.9 to 11.5.10.2, this was a version skip which we regression-tested and feature-tested for months, to assure all critical business systems would function fine after the upgrade.

We had (and I was responsible for) a massive Microsoft Project Plan. It was a thing of glory — hundreds of lines, loads of start-to-finish and finish-to-start dependencies. Tasks were allocated and milestones were defined. What it lacked in accuracy it made up for in pageantry. Speaking of pageantry, the status reports and status meetings were the Belle of the Ball! Weekly we'd meet and review a two-slide status report. It only shaded amber when we wanted to make a team move faster than they were, but held strong at green for the majority of the project. The entire project took about six months from start to finish. Each month, waterfalling into the next.

As November approached, I knew the cutover from version 11.5.9 to version 11.5.10.2 was nearing. We had targeted Thanksgiving weekend as that allows for a four-day outage in the United States. We had done a number of dry runs, so we clocked the time needed to do the full system back up (RMAN), the upgrade process itself, the additional features we were deploying along with the upgrade, and the requisite testing. We also had a set timing for the backout plan if required, but we had done so many Oracle upgrades in this exact pattern so many times without issue, the backout plan seemed comical. The first backup script was to fire off at 21:00, EST on (Wednesday before Thanksgiving 2006). I remember being on that initiation call, and working through the first shift of scripts, all while updating my project plan for go live. Every four hours I would send the status email to the project team, and CC the CIO himself. As expected, all the work was going according to plan. Somewhere around 02:00 my shift ended, and I tried to catch some sleep. I had steps to do in the morning around the core upgrade itself, and really needed a few solid hours of REM sleep, but the adrenaline of my first major release was fighting with the serotonin in my body — I hardly slept at all. Working from home, I made a little camp in my basement near my office so that even when I was sleeping I was close to everything I needed.

When I woke the next morning, I made a fresh pot of coffee, made sure the turkey for Thanksgiving went in the oven, and got back to jamming on my trusty IBM Thinkpad. Much to my delight, the upgrade was still rocking along to plan! Around noon, I remember us doing the smoke tests which comprised of some simple features, transactions and an innocuous data comparison. That data test just ensured the data that was in the tablespace prior to the 11.5.10.2 upgrade was still there post. We had run this at least three to four times prior in the lower environments, each time it passed. This time, in production, as my turkey cooked and my family was showing up to start watching football and eat, something unique happened. It failed. There was less data in the new tablespaces than in the old. During the upgrade, we lost data. But that cannot be. We tested this, a number of times. We followed the documented migration path. We did all the right things, damnit!

The next six hours are honestly a blur. I know we had a hotline open with Oracle support. I know I had calls coming into my (super sweet) Nextel mobile from folks whose names I had only seen high up on the org chart, and never spoken to live before. I also know that we made the call to backout the upgrade and use the Oracle migration utility again, to try to reinstall 10.5.10.2 again, hoping a step was missed and a fresh reinstall would fix the data issue. Once that call was made, we signed a fictitious contract to power though at least 12 hours of new work, er — re-work. At this point, I had a family eating in my dining room, discussing all they were thankful for in that year, while I am in my basement pacing and tearing out my 26-year-old hair (yes, I did have hair at that time). As this was my project, I was under the microscope. I had to make a call to the CIO every 30 minutes at the top and the bottom of the hour to give an update, even if the update was "no update." It was brutal. I remember forcing myself to stand because I was afraid I would fall asleep if I sat down. At this point, I had effectively slept 1.5 hours in the past 36. And there was no sign that a real sleep was coming anytime soon. As Thursday switched over to Friday, we finished the reinstallation. We ran the smoke tests again, and all I wanted to see was a different result than we had seen the day before. Sadly, I got my wish. No, we didn't find out the data issue went away, we found out it got worse. More data was missing this time. FFS.

If things were tense before, we just went into the North Korea level of tension. Finger pointing and blame took over what I had previously thought were some of the top technical minds I had met to date. We went back to the Oracle support team and found ourselves in a priority status that we had not heard of before, some super high "drop all other shit" status level. We spoke to several core Oracle support and engineering leads. At this point, we spoke to a gentleman named Mohammad based in Egypt. He was an on-call support person, that happened to be pulled in. He was far from the senior folks we all were locked in on hoping praying they would find a solution to this situation. Mohammad dug into the logs, asked for a copy of our backed up data and disappeared. As we thrashed on the Oracle support call, and slung half brained theories on what we could do via instant messenger, Mohammad hammered out a script. He seemed to have found a small issue somewhere between our data and the migration scripts that likely would cause a race condition, so he added a patch to the script to handle the error.

After some interesting conversation about the validity of both Mohammad's error hypothesis and the effectiveness of his script, we agreed to re-install, a third time, using this patched script. Given the time required to install the whole upgrade, we made the decision to split the team, so we could install simultaneously in production and to the non-production, staging environment. Given the time required to install in staging, then again in production, we would have breached the drop dead time for the upgrade to be completed, without impacting critical business process scheduled for Sunday evening such as customer billing and end of month batch processing. As the fresh install was coming to an end, my sheer exhaustion was shifting to optimism. I was starting to blindly trust we were heading to a happy ending, again we had never failed on a major release. In the non-production, staging environment, we completed the install faster, because it had far less data than production. We ran the smoke tests and everything passed. But that meant very little since everything had passed there prior to Mohammad's patch. Some time later, production was re-installed with the patched script. On a call with five people, I remember waiting to hear the result of the smoke test live. Each test slowly came back as passing. Then we reached the data comparison test. It was likely a five-minute test at most, but it felt like an eternity. And then my lead DBA spoke in a faint accented voice and said, "it passed." In a somber, monotone voice, he said the two words I wanted to hear most in the world! We then started to mobilize everyone. The functional testers, the business team, the CIO (of course) and then the compliance team to let them know we had cleared the blockage. Or so we thought.

You see, as a regulated enterprise company, we were required to maintain Sarbanes-Oxley compliance. In order to allow Mohammad's script to live in production, specifically because it related to PII data, we had to demonstrate the appropriate levels of segregation of duty and testing of the script and data in the lower environments. And, frankly speaking, we didn't have the time to do those tests in staging. As we discussed what options we had, our drop dead time approached. We were going to breach the drop dead at this point, nothing we could do would allow for the functional and acceptance tests to complete in production now. They were all manual, even if there were no issues at all, they would not be done in time. That Saturday evening or Sunday morning I made the call to reverse the upgrade. Restore the RMAN backup. Reset the entire production environment back to a state like it was on Wednesday evening, the end of the business day in California. We completed and tested the backout on schedule, and allowed for the business critical processes to run Sunday evening. We failed to upgrade production.

Compliance as code was, at best, in its infancy in 2006. It certainly was not a reality at the enterprise at which I worked. Modern build/test/deploy pipelines are being built to allow for the most simple of compliance checks, to the extreme, to be represented as injectable rules. Monitoring systems provide a feedback loop to the health of the change and the overall system in near real time. Had this been in place at my company in 2006 for this upgrade, we could have very quickly asserted the Sarbanes-Oxley compliance checkpoints. But it wasn't, so we couldn't. But here we are, 14 years later.

I now consult for large enterprises on how to better enable healthy systems and build elite teams. Very few of these enterprises have ANY compliance as code framework in place!. There are an army of vendors and tools that will line up to offer you the blue pill (or is it the red?) to solve this with a license, but to me, the epic failure in this state for most all enterprises is the resistance to partner the compliance organization with the engineering organization. There is a visceral distance in some organizations between these groups that prevents doing what is right for the company, the users and the intent of the regulation itself. As the new, digital-first cohort of leaders come to board rooms and executive meetings, it is imperative to not only address this divide, but close it ASAP.

Envy

Perhaps the most egregious of all DevSecOps sins is the belief that tooling will save you. Mark Miller and I have had friendly discussions about this in the past. One of my core beliefs is that security must be embedded into the culture of any successful team/organization. Too often, security leaders fall into the trap of looking at white papers or marketing materials from vendors about how their peers or competition are securing their systems with various tools. Using simple correlation, you can leap to the conclusion that a team's security posture is a result of the tooling. And, trust me, the tools are the commodity. The bespoke item in secure teams is the security mindset and capabilities. There is a saying "Treat your keys like underwear, never let anyone see them and change them often." This speaks to my point. Be aware of best practices and be rigorous enough to stay one step ahead of the bad actors, rather than obsessing with what your contemporaries are doing.

Sure, be alert and aware of what is going on in the market. Stay current with NIST policy changes. Watch which commercial tools are coming into the market to secure the most recent tech. But first and foremost, build out a DevSecOps mindset and community of practice within your walls.

One of the largest US financial services companies, well known for their progressive, early adoption of the cloud and modern take on DevSecOps had a very unique position on internal upskilling during their rapid journey atop the technology ladder. They created an in-house university. This group has a remit to "put the employees in the driver's seat," but the reality is they are shifting capabilities such as security, automation, quality, and provisioning left by making an active investment towards the capability uplift of the team, and attaching that to annual incentives. So if there is one group to be envious of, it is the one that actively invests in security capabilities and DevOps best practices within itself.

About Ryan Lockard

Ryan is a Vice President with Contino, a global Enterprise DevOps, Data and Cloud Transformation Consultancy. He has nearly 20 years experience leading organizations and teams through transformative change. Ryan has a proven record making ROI driven change in Financial Services, Health Care, Telecommunications and Manufacturing verticals. His experience from both inside the enterprise and rapid growth in consulting has made him uniquely positioned for success and growth via a stern focus on data driven outcomes to demonstrate ROI to clients. Ryan has led large scale transformations in some of the most heavily regulated customers in the world, earning himself trust and partnership with the client C-Suite as a trusted advisor and executive coach.

He is a lifelong Philadelphia resident, father of three, and always interested in a conversation about good craft beer or coffee.

Acknowledgments

Thank you to my beautiful wife, Emma. You stay at home so I can travel the world pretending to be a smart guy.

REFERENCES

» www.en.m.wikipedia.org/wiki/Kubernetes

» www.whitehouse.gov/wp-content/uploads/2017/11/FY2017FISMAReportCongress.pdf

» www.congress.gov/bill/116th-congress/senate-bill/1790

DEV
SEC
OPS
DAYS

CHAPTER 8

Did You Try Turning It Off and On?

How Simple Bugs Lead to Serious Defects & Vulnerabilities

by Chris Riley

CHAPTER 8
Did You Try Turning It Off And On?
How Simple Bugs Lead to
Serious Defects & Vulnerabilities

It all began with the CEO being unable to send an email. Back in the day, Lotus Notes was the king, and applications ran on hunks of steel, not virtual machines. One day, at one of the worlds largest tech companies, the inability of approximately 13,000 employees to send and receive email was the catalyst for sheer panic. The culprit was a light switch. Names have been changed to protect the mostly innocent.

Bill was on call. It was 1995, and the best notification method, at that time, for being on-call was a brick of a pager. Bill's company was not willing to invest in cell phones. Email, in this case, was out of the question. It was a calm week, and a smooth Friday. Bill finished his week by doing the rounds at the data center after racking a new box for a DB2 backend. When Bill's work was done he was eager to head out and to start the weekend with a hot date. Shortly after he had picked up his date, he received a page. His date thought it was a drug deal, but he knew it was a different sort of trouble. Apparently the executive assistant of the CEO called the director of IT, who looked at an on-call spreadsheet naming Bill as the victim. This was not the typical process. Usually there were many more hoops, but at the time, the key stakeholder was able to escalate the situation with ease. The best option for Bill was to pull over, locate the nearest phone booth, and call in. He was greeted with, "Bill, the CEO can't send emails, what's going on?"

In 1995 the criteria for being a Jr. IT Manager was as easy as taking one computer science course, and showing an aptitude. Bill enjoyed his computer science class, and he was ready to enter the real world of IT. At this time there was also a massive move from mainframe applications to a client-server. Little did Bill know that he was going to get the keys to a massive datacenter, previously a hardware assembly plant, where mainframe to client-server migration had just taken place, and everyone was flying just a little blind.

If you are a Jr. IT manager like Bill, and get this call, everything puckers up. There is no way not to feel guilt and pressure to get things solved. During this time, the blameless culture did not exist and outages nearly always had an internal victim with long-term consequences.

Back to the datacenter Bill went, and fast. When he got there to check the Lotus server, he noticed that it had recently restarted and was in the process of booting up. Problem solved? Not the definition of self healing most hoped for, but it did explain the outage, and hopefully the restart was the solution. A moderately equipped Lotus server at the time took a good 30 minutes to be up and available. After 30 minutes, email was up and running, but the root cause was not yet clear. After doing some digging in the logs there was no clear indication of what was going on. There were no flood of errors just prior to the reboot. Bill did not want to lose sight of what was most important at that time, his date! He decided that this was all he could do for now and chalked it up to some fluke reboot. This is where an experienced IT would have known that things were just beginning.

Bill made a note to troubleshoot next week and got back on the road. Fifteen minutes later, another page. Instead of finding a phone booth, he went straight to the datacenter and picked up the phone, "Bill, it's down again." What was going on? Not only was the Lotus server rebooting again, so was every machine on that particular rack, but none of them showed obvious errors to justify the reboot. Without clear indication it was something with the server itself, and not related to the other servers which also restarted, all that was left was power. Bill turned to look at the wall, and there it was. The light switch right by the door with a slip of blue painters tape dangling in defeat. That switch was the bug and the tape a very poor safety mechanism. That particular rack was mistakenly on a switched outlet intended for extra lighting and Bill had flipped the switch. Twice.

When the next week rolled around this particular case had high visibility, and the post mortem was a key asset to figuring out a long term solution. Don't use switched outlets and invest in auxiliary power. The post mortem looked something like this:

Lotus Server Periodic Power Loss
Nov 10, 1995 5:45 PM – Nov 10, 1989 8:30 PM

Timeline
5:45 pm – Initial report via page & acknowledged
6:15 pm – Server automatically rebooted
6:45 pm – Systems green services running
6:50 pm – Issue noted for further investigation
7:10 pm – Issue reappeared, reported, & acknowledged
7:30 pm – Server automatically rebooted again
8:00 pm – Systems green services running
8:10 pm – Root cause identified

Action Notes
- Notice un-expected restart
- Checked server logs, no anomalies
- Waited for restart and verified email service is running

Root Cause
Server rack was mistakenly on switched outlet. The tape on light switch noting this was defective and not visible. Switch was inadvertently switched off twice, disrupting power to the rack, and disabling the Lotus Notes server.

Resolution
Remove server from switched outlet, remove all switched outlets.

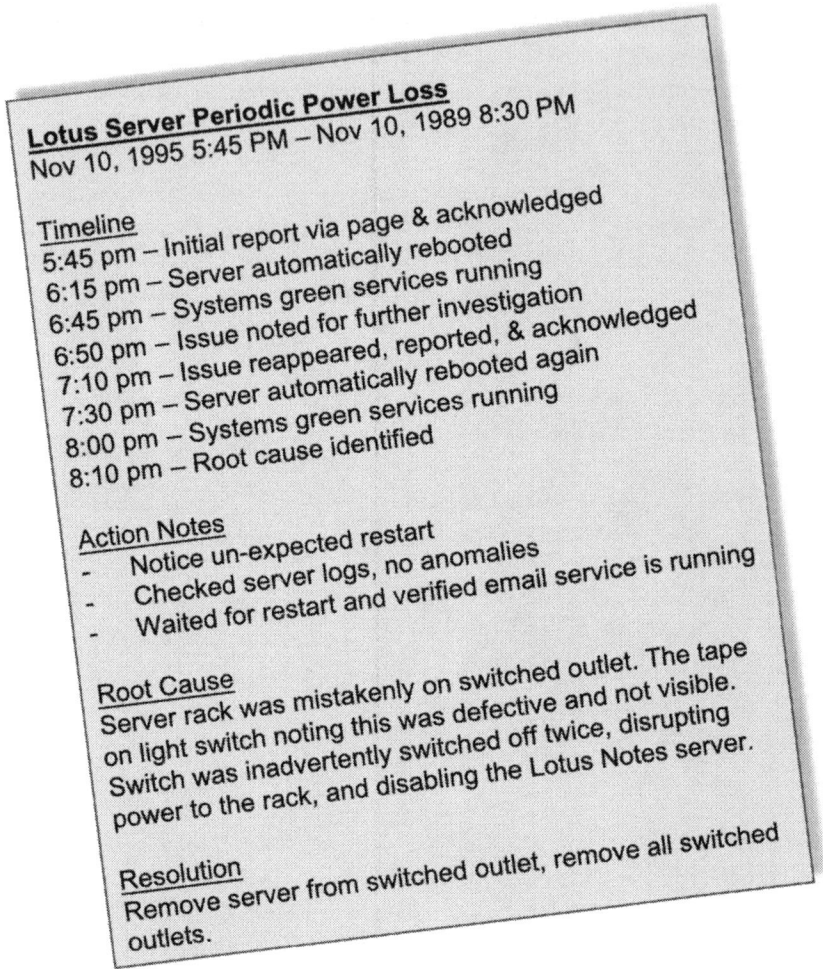

While it was not a permanent fix, the short term fix was a mound of tape on the light switch and a sign that said, "DO NOT TURN OFF." The runbook for future incidents, in this case, would be to turn the power back on. It was so simple. But the impact of the lost emails on a multinational company was tremendous and not trivial. Not only was it a threat to the business operation but it was a clear path for any would be saboteur.

Bill was lucky that no drives were lost and everything came back up after a hard power cycle. But this incident left him feeling stupid, left the IT organization embarrassed, and an entire company with lost emails. The level of redundancy that we have today, did not exist back then, thus a days worth of lost emails created many issues. It was an undue risk, with potential revenue loss, compliance and lost efficiency.

There is clearly a major flaw in your infrastructure if someone can take it down with the flip of a switch. Where was the UPS? In Bill's case this was a physical switch, but many switches that are as simple to toggle and as widely exposed still exist in every tier of an application.

Step One: Turn Off, Step Two: Turn On

If you are in IT or unintentional IT for your family, you have used the "off/on" solution many times to solve computer issues. Sometimes it's your default answer even before doing any sort of discovery. In Bill's case however the off/on was unintentional. What is so amazing about this story is how something as simple as a binary flip of a switch can take down a business' critical systems, and incite a ton of fear. The outcomes of the bug were much more dramatic than the complexity of it.

I enjoy this story for so many reasons. First, at Bill's expense, it's hilarious. Second, because it's retro. We know now that no datacenter would ever be setup this way, but back then data centers were just places to store and plug things in. What nerd doesn't like to talk about the good ol' days. The story also highlights the big impact of seemingly innocuous problems. During those days of IT, things were more rudimentary than they are today, which made understanding what was going on even easier. Modern applications and infrastructure have become more complex with many more moving parts. The ratio of simplicity to the magnitude of impact is fun and worth exploring in modern day instances.

Engineers love to talk about the KISS (Keep It Simple Stupid) principle, but they rarely follow it since engineers spend most of their time grappling with large problems. Thus, when something breaks, we expect it to be equally complex. The semicolon was the death of my development career building Optical Character Recognition (OCR) engines and Genetic Algorithm (GA) SDKs. The fact that I could prevent a compile of any code with a single missed character within large chunks of complex algorithms, drove me nuts. I was either to be committed, or admit coding was not for me.

Turning things off and on seems funny, but still in many outages it is a common catalyst for issues. We just use different language to describe it, rollback, re-route, and flags. Many of the runbooks written today are scripts filled with methods for rolling back services. If it's not a rollback it could literally be restarting an instance that is pegged, or cleaning up drive space. Essentially, often the problem and the solution are fairly basic. However, the impact of these basic issues can be dramatic and ironically we may not even be spending time on the root cause as it seems too trivial to be the solution.

The Relationship Between Switches and Security

In a microservices world, toggles are everywhere. Toggles increase the attack surface for applications and infrastructure. The benefit of toggles is the ability to support self-serve and the scripted nature of modern infrastructure and software delivery chains, which is a huge gain for modern operations, and arguably the only way to keep up with the velocity of new code. But it also means that there are more entry points. While the potential exploits found at the intersection of digital toggles and public access to them generally are not a catalyst for the highest severity breaches, their volume, and clever relationships between the toggles and the code do make them a common and relatively easy place for hackers to start. If the motive is to disrupt operation, then it is the easiest path.

Besides microservices, another place where this is manifesting in an exponential way is with REST APIs. API first development is more and more common, especially for teams building platforms where other services are reliant on each other and the simplest form of integration is a well documented API. The problem is a subset of these APIs often become the basis for the public version. A very public example of this occurred in July of 2017 when Facebook introduced a new bug into their API which exposed the data of 50 million users leveraging single-sign-on tokens, demonstrating that a simple post with the right parameters can be catastrophic.

Toggle Safely

Bill's light switch is a basic toggle. Toggles have become increasingly more complex in the application and IT world, and are found everywhere, including being instrumented in code, and in scripted infrastructure. The virtual switches have the same impact as the physical one.

There is no stopping the spread of toggles, nor should organizations aim to do so. Without the flexibility that smaller, switchable, and more portable chunks of code provide we would be moving in the opposite direction of application features and velocity. The monolith is the exact definition of this, and in Bill's case the monolith included the server, and the power it was connected to. That is it.

So get limiting toggles out of your mind and, in fact, be ready to increase application integrity and security by introducing more. The best way to frame a strategy to address the modern digital switch problem is more testing, smarter design patterns, better monitoring, and better alerts.

Continuous Testing

Anticipating that toggles in the application will change, potentially even in production, is an important thing to acknowledge, but also not fight. The trick is being aware of when this happens, and the potential impact of an off/on. Classically when applications end up in production, the monitoring is limited to the basic traffic coming in and infrastructure up time. While this increases awareness on the big buckets, such as the plug being pulled, it does not address the complexities of modern applications. That is why teams need to keep testing beyond deployment, extending the test automation into production. There you can have a test suite that will continuously poke at the application in production so that any inadvertent changes to code, rollbacks, feature flags, artifacts, and infrastructure changes are visible and their impact known. Because a test suite goes beyond up/down status it is able to reach a more critical depth of understanding by checking for the relationship of components and the functionality they support. Continuous testing should include:

» Ongoing vulnerability scanning

» Ongoing functional test automation

» Ongoing unit testing

» Contracts

Contract testing is the big one. Microservices applications and application architectures where individual services teams may never utter a word to others is where the toggles can be complicated and how the API functions, matters a lot. Contract testing is the process of testing the expected communication between services. It's a contract that one service team makes with another on what they input and what they output, in specific ways. If you are going to instrument a service that relates to another service, these contracts are essential to building your functionality. Also in test automation, make sure that as services are they continue to play nice with each other and if your contract has a flag/toggle/switch with an expected state, that it is actually delivered. Microservices very often have their own lifecycle, so in addition to not being able to communicate directly about functionality, teams are not always aware of where a service is in it's latest incarnation. They should not need to, or they need to delay their functionality because a related service is not done with theirs.

If you are super brave, you can and should also include the chaos test. Flip those switches for funsies. Kill a pod, toggle a feature, rollback services, just to see what happens. Sounds scary, but chaos will happen, and it can be automatically generated in a manageable and visible way.

Smarter Design Patterns

Being smarter about the design patterns development teams use simply means considering how you build applications beyond core functionality. The pillars of being smarter about your application design is that best practices are created and used team wide, and they are evaluated against how they help or hurt application quality and potential risk. Normally we talk about design patterns as they relate to functionality only.

This is also because modern applications are not far removed from their infrastructure, and with Kubernetes and containers they are basically one in the same. Design patterns impact the application at all tiers now. Organizations need to consider how they build their applications and standardize design best practices across the team. This standardization does a lot of things in terms of making applications easier to test, easier to understand when things break, and better correlate the relationship between various components.

The goals we are trying to achieve with better design patterns are more isolation, mitigated failure impact, faster failure identification, and faster resolution. These are what the below suggestions are based on.

 » **Contracts:** Contracts are essentially a documented promise between microservices on how that service will communicate with all others. It is both an example of a design pattern and a practice.

» **Self-Documenting APIs:** People hate creating docs, but love complaining about bad documentation. Not all documentation can be automatically generated, but with APIs in particular they can be. Good documentation helps communication between teams, helps resolve issues, but also creates a layer of visibility that can spot potential exposure points in APIs. The trick with documentation, and the benefit of automated docs is brevity. You should not say more than is needed to use functionality, but you also can't be too short.

» **Be Stateless and Event Based:** Without states you don't necessarily have a switch to be flipped or at least one that is scoped to the entire application. I am not implying that stateless architectures are a bulletproof firewall, but it does limit the impact of bad requests and forces a completeness in adoption and creation. Being stateless and/or event based also forces the services layer to be the lens for the entire application.

» **Test Driven Development:** Write your functional tests before you write the feature. The nice thing about contributing to a book like this is that I get to be prescriptive for things that I myself would not do. But this is also why no one should hire me as a developer. Test driven development feels like you are being punished even before you did anything wrong. I get it. But the feeling of success once you do complete the feature, and it passes the unit test is tremendous. The big thing that you gain with test driven development practices is a buffer. Tactically you are doing a better job at validating the features you write. But it also creates a bugger for the developer before they crank out new code. They will think about that code's impact on the overall code base and surface areas, where it might cause problems, be it functionality, potential vulnerabilities, or breaks in internal best practice. Unit tests should be seen beyond just their functional test value.

» **Bulkhead Pattern:** As it relates to microservices applications, the bulkhead pattern helps tremendously when identifying if something breaks. This is where you partition functionality into groups. The hard part is determining the information architecture of those groups such that it makes sense, and is not just redundant for the services themselves. The groups should have a relation to infrastructure, where as services generally relate to functionality. The groups should be determined in advance, and not during the processes of development.

» **Sidecar Pattern:** A happy companion of bulkhead is the sidecar. With the sidecar you attach features to broader applications. Arguably this is just microservices, but it is instrumented such that a sidecar can actually be linked to the services like a parasite. It offers similar logical isolation as bulkhead pattern, but in this case can actually be used in remediation. It helps contain the fall out of a vulnerability, but forces more effort on the overall architecture planning.

» **Robust API Gateway:** If you allow your services a lot of flexibility, but have your API gateway as an overall control plane for all communication, you can build safety nets into the API gateway to prevent basic changes causing catastrophic events. It's almost a monolithic communication overlay on a non-monolithic application.

While it's not really a design pattern but just a good practice, development teams should be continuously refactoring their code to remove outdated and unused code blocks or validating that new code written does not duplicate something that already exists. This is extremely important and good developer hygiene. Easier said than done. This has to be systematized through the development team, and it also has to include your test suite. In your test suite, not only are you wasting a huge amount of time running tests on functionality that is no longer used, you are exposing its existence.

Do not write a new function that is a ctl+v of another where you are just making incremental changes. It may feel like it will take you longer to understand an older function to update, than to just recreate it, but the risk of abandoning it and it becoming an issue later is a far greater pain. Just don't be lazy. Before diving into new code, make sure it does not deprecate old. If it does, get rid of the old. Test driven development can also help identify this, but it can't force the habit, it has to be standardized across the team.

Better Monitoring

For the longest time application performance monitoring and infrastructure monitoring have been a process of record, and move on. At least move on until something breaks, much like documentation monitoring was treated as a "set it and forget it" until it's needed practice. As development teams evolve into DevOps practices they are seeing monitoring as a more proactive tool, and even a tool for self healing.

In the world of cyber security, monitoring is pretty mature. Security Event and

Incident Management (SEIMs) are a set of well known tooling and practices. The same practices fit within DevSecOps but what is tremendously different is that the end-points are not just servers and devices, they are snippets of code. The vulnerabilities found in applications go deep. And the deeper they are the harder they are to discover. So monitoring needs to be top down from client to app as well as inside out from code to client. This is where modern monitoring tools come in.

There is a new generation of monitoring, and it has introduced concepts like distributed tracing, and observability. The other radical change is that monitoring is being done on streams of data versus logs. This introduces a new set of overhead for infrastructure and applications, but also a very necessary set of visibility.

Development teams need to understand two key things about monitoring their applications.

» The tools are only as good as the information architecture that has been established for the data they ingest. Information architecture is how information is organized from sources to tags. But also how it is consumed, from dashboards to individual access.

» The tools are only as good as their instrumentation. If you want full visibility you need to instrument your monitoring at the code level up. I wish there was an uber agent that could pry into every nook and cranny of applications, but generally developers need to take monitoring to the next level by introducing specific tools that can monitor at the code and API level.

The basis of monitoring tools is the same; collect some data, show some data. But they have become more and more specialized in the way they collect and display information. Concepts like real-user monitoring (RUM) and exception monitoring have entered the market as more code-level monitoring approaches, as well as distributed tracing for more modern infrastructures. At the end of the day a good monitoring tool can be manipulated into covering your entire stack, but finding a good vendor partner that can help you get there in the most comprehensive way is important.

The other trend with monitoring is the ability of monitoring tools to take on first-tier remediation. This is starting the trend of self healing. Tools can now run scripts to solve common issues such as shutting down vulnerable services, or doing a rollback. While this functionality is not a requirement, it soon will be, and it is good to plan for it.

Machine learning is also a new and common term thrown in the monitoring conversation. There is intelligence regularly being built into monitoring tools by some really smart data scientists. It is not the singularity and it's not magic. Where it is being deployed has very clear problem/solution value. Don't expect magic when you hear "machine learning," but realize there are tactical use cases, and it's better to focus on the use case than the term.

Using terms like self healing, machine learning, and distributed tracing are cool party tricks, and they also provide real value.

Better Alerts

Like monitoring, most alerting is considered the process of barking. Like Bill's page. Alerting is not just about being loud to the people who need to know. It has a lot to do with context, and everything mentioned above are ways to build more context. Continuous testing gives more coverage, better design patterns give more detail and better monitoring gives humans greater visibility when something goes wrong. The next step is taking action.

The typical alerting scenario is this. You get the call because you are on a spreadsheet, you acknowledge something bad has happened, then you go call your favorite dev to help you fix it. There is this path of least resistance we establish, often at the burn-out cost of our team mates. But modern incident response and management should get alerts to the right person based on intelligence, giving the responder great context to address an alert. Things like access to a runbook, monitoring tool dashboards, and full traces. And then help them track and audit the entire process of remediation, or bringing other subject matter experts into the fire fight.

Bill in this case was alone, he was junior and under a lot of pressure from his employer and his girlfriend. What modern tooling could have done for Bill was let him know that it was not just the Lotus server that went unresponsive, it was several, all on the same rack. Access to monitoring tools would have let him know that nothing strange was happening on any of the boxes up to the point of failure. This should have been sufficient for him to realize that power might have been the root cause. Now in the world of IT the Universal Power Supply (UPS) could also have thrown an alert, if they used them.

People Have Switches Too

Bill was to blame for flipping a light switch, but how did that rack get on a switched outlet to begin with? Obviously, the person who made that decision at the time did not feel like they would be affected by it. Surely they knew it was not the best idea? Probably faster then running new power to the newly added rack at the end of the row. A spur of the moment decision that did not include the team.

Ah the people problem, the most frustrating aspect of DevOps adoption. I rarely run into people who simply do not want to collaborate and are still on team silo. But no matter how well intentioned your team is, including you, when you get in the thick of application development, testing, delivery, and support, over communicating is not a top priority. Our first inclination is to look to tools (is teamwork a thing?) to help, techies are notorious for secretly wanting to be robots and reducing everything to if/then statements. People, because of this crazy thing called emotions and ego, are not willing to fit into an algorithm.

The best system I have found is to adopt Maslow's Hierarchy of Needs into a decision hierarchy of needs where no decision can be made until the previous need is met. The first filter for every decision is communication. Can you answer the following:

» Does this change impact a specific function/team that is out of your direct influence?

» Who/what does it impact?

» How should you best communicate the change to the owners/influencers of the impacted function/team?

The first question is easy to answer, except for the fact that you can be overly inclusive and make a case for every change impacting the entire team. You have to be discerning and always reverse back from the applications/services impacted. The last question is the hardest. Because one of the biggest deterrents of long term effective communication is when someone believes they have already communicated effectively, but finds out later that communication went nowhere, and they have to repeat themselves.

The repetition problem. Most people hate to repeat themselves, and you should. The more you spend time repeating yourself, the less time you spend on higher value tasks. But if someone does not listen to the message you deliver, then you will have no choice. Applications are developed in a very utilitarian world and all that matters is the outcome.

So the first filter in the Hierarchy of Decision Needs is the hardest to pass and the most time consuming. Just like in documentation, the goal should be brevity. If the communication does not deliver clear value or insight, then it should not be given. This takes a lot of personality out of the equation, but that is the erratic factor you are trying to control for. It should not impact the character of your team or your culture that the communication outside of getting code shipped is casual.

ChatOps is a technology that has stepped in to help and has become a tremendous tool, as long as it does not just become a modern version of a broken system. The benefit of ChatOps is the tools force fast and brief messages. The team needs to be skilled in crafting these messages, and making sure they are clear. If they are effective at doing so, then the ratio of shared information to repeated information will drop naturally. So there is an incentive to do so. As ChatOps evolves the addition of intelligent bots that retrieve historical communication based on new questions of the team could be tremendous in avoiding repetition.

If the team can act like robots when it's required to ship and manage applications and as humans when it comes to collaborating, then the bi-modal operation can be super efficient. As more and more automation becomes available, automating the tasks make it so there is one less thing to potentially have bad communication around. Don't let bad communication and the people problem become a good justification to avoid DevOps and embrace the monolith.

Modern Digital Light Switch

There is no way to prevent the digital light switch from surfacing. Code bases are large, fragmented and ever more complex. The idea is to leverage tooling and best practices to know how to respond faster and resolve faster.

We have not really advanced beyond the light switch. There are light switches all over our code and infrastructure. One of my new favorite ones is Feature Flags. This is a super powerful design pattern. Feature flags is the ability to turn on or off features on demand. Sound familiar. A similar incident to the physical switch occurs when a feature flag which other features were later dependent on is flipped off.

An example in the real world is a new feature that gives users the ability to add items from a wishlist to a shopping cart. Once this feature was turned on an element of it was tied to the cart itself, creating a direct relationship between the new feature and the existing one, the shopping cart service.

At some point the product team decided that this feature was not where they wanted it to be. It lacked adoption and there were plans for making it much more robust by linking it to analytics that would drive users to move wishlist items to the cart as quickly as possible. When they decided on this they leveraged the power of feature flags to turn the feature off in production. The problem was that now the checkout button in the cart was intimately linked to this feature, such that if there were any items in the cart that were currently or at some point on a user's wishlist, the user could no longer check out. Exceptions were collecting as users tried to check out, there was an abnormally high amount of cart abandonment and support was overwhelmed with tickets. The first place the the team checked was the backend, next the codebase for the shopping cart service, then all the checkout functions. But the solution was as easy as a switch turned off.

You could argue that in this case there was a flaw in deciding feature boundaries. You could also see how the sidecar pattern could have been a big help. But... *would of, should of.* This is going to happen in your code base, kill switch landmines. The answer is not to stop using feature flags, or stop allowing them to be toggled in production. The answer is to know how to respond to issues, have a mechanism that gives visibility into this manual change, and understand that the issue really could be that simple.

Framing for the Inevitable Kill Switch

Someone in the next year will flip a switch that will take down a significant portion of your application or expose your application to undue risk. It's going to happen. So the team shouldn't pretend it won't. The organization should have confidence in knowing how they will address the problem.

> » First off, the KISS principle applies to incident response as well. The team should know to not overreact or over assume the issue is something more complex that it actually is. Techies like to be problem solvers and when the alarm bells go off we can often go into John Nash mode and over complicate the issue. Until you can validate that it isn't, leave the possibility open for the

issue to be trivial and basic. Establish a procedure for high-level sanity checks and go through it quickly. Is the power on? Is this an external access issue? For example, try pinging relevant services and running health checks. Ideally your monitoring tool will have done this for you already, as there is a good chance this is the source of the alert anyway.

» Next, establish an escalation policy that is meaningful and efficient, not just convenient. So many organizations get complacent, for good reason, when an alert happens. They will call the one person who can fix everything, they will avoid reading runbooks, and they will address the symptoms without spending the time to identify the cause. In modern systems when one thing breaks, often times so do many other things. Once you acknowledge an alert, expect more. There is a good chance it's all related. It's important to triage the incident to understand the root cause, because often times the root cause is not the initial system that screamed at you.

» Once the root cause is established, be laser focused on remediating that issue.

» When the systems come back up, you are not done. Often times you can get things back up and running by failover of the affected services, but there could be other issues. The flood of errors can pile on for a while and things like performance can be impacted. Understand your steady state, have a way of measuring it and look for the steady state before you consider all things good.

You might think the answer is simply, "do not have switched outlets," i.e. don't have literal kill switches in your code. However trivial that seems at scale with massive code bases this is actually something pretty difficult to expect. Things will break. Having an understanding of how your team will approach it is not only important to build consistency in responding to issues and spotting trivial issues faster. It's also important so that the organization is not built on a team of institutional knowledge, where any changes in the team have a direct impact on the response rate and mean time to recovery.

"Bill, CEO Still Can't Send Email"

Bill's story is fun because we can reminisce about old technology, judge the ridiculous infrastructure, and laugh about his plight. The reality is, something your team is doing today will be just as trivial and hilarious in 20 years. So, embrace acceptance: the acceptance that you are not as advanced as you think you are, you are not as DevOps as you think you are, and you are not immune to trivial bugs.

We have made huge strides in automation, monitoring, and alerting since then, but there is more to come. Bill heard about the issue from the entire organization, the CEO's executive assistant in particular had a lot to say. This was not a time of blameless culture and the infrastructure was setup in an unstable way.

Bill was on the hook. The aggressor of the Lotus outage now has an amazing career as a … Sales Director. That's right. And, "the date" later became his wife.

Ultimately, IT wasn't for Bill, who now has an amazing career as a Sales Director of an enterprise software company. That is how I learned his story, as he was training a team on the very real day-to-day problems techies face. Bill can now talk with pure empathy to any techie who is or was on call at some point and knows the feeling of business critical systems being down where the solution is stupid obvious. Bill is now a tech hero trying to mitigate and address these techie life challenges. Fortunately for Bill his date did not only stick around after an annoying distraction to their evening, she is now his wife of 20+ years. We all survive the major outages, but by being effective in knowing how we will deal with them versus avoiding them, our lives, and the lives of our team, will be better and applications more stable and secure.

About Chris Riley

Chris Riley (@hoardinginfo) is obsessed with bringing modern technologies to those who need to solve real-world problems, going from unicorn to reality.

Chris speaks and engages with end-users regularly in the areas of DevOps, SecOps, and App Dev. He works for Splunk as a Tech Advocate and is a regular contributor to industry blogs such as ContainerJournal.com, DevOps.com and Sweetcode.io. He is also the host of the podcast, Developers Eating the World.

As a bad-coder-turned-technology-advocate, Chris understands the challenges and needs of modern engineers, as well as how technology fits into the broader business goals of companies in a demanding high-tech world.

Chris obtained his Computer Science and Business degrees from Regis University in Colorado and currently lives in Colorado with his wife and two daughters. He is a fan of physics and psychology, and has an eclectic set of hobbies that range from Genetic Algorithms (GA) to Mineral Collecting to LEGO.

Acknowledgments

Often times the best stories and knowledge transfer come from a stream of consciousness. It takes an army, in my case especially, to make that stream sound good. I want to thank all the copy editors, and practitioner proofreaders for taking the time to review and beautify my thoughts. I also want to thank a certain coworker who made the meat of this story very real.

DEV
SEC
OPS
DAYS

CHAPTER 9

Kill the Restructure

by Rob England
and
Dr. Cherry Vu

CHAPTER 9

Kill the Restructure

There are new ways of working and managing that are a better way. We can make work better, faster, cheaper, safer, and happier. The word isn't getting out fast enough. There are classic mistakes being made over and over, as large organisations try to "do Agile/DevOps/MagicNewWay," "implement Agile/DevOps," or — *shudder* — "transform."

Advance Not Transform

We should avoid the word "transform." (Although old habits die hard and I still catch myself using it.) "Transformation" is done by fairy godmothers. Or caterpillars. Large entities don't change like that: they don't change that fast, and it isn't a finite step. We say "advance."

Let's list some of the more dysfunctional approaches to advancing Agile culture:

» Big bang change.

» Change done *to* people instead of improvement done *by* people.

» "Transformation" as a finite project.

» Expectation that culture can change quickly.

» Treating culture as a simple system not a complex one.

» Belief that management know the answers.

» Starting with a restructure.

» *Only* doing a restructure.

Most of all: failure to change the management and governance. This is perhaps the biggest issue of them all. Management is the lock on advancement. The primary function of many middle managers is to control risk. They're change-resistant by nature. Add to that senior management who are blissfully unaware of their own need to change, and advancement is going nowhere.

Complex System

Work is a complex system. It's an organic soup of attitudes, beliefs, behaviours, mood, vision, personalities... There are no crisp inputs and outputs, just energy and activity in a network. You don't know how to change it. Nobody knows, no matter how much you pay them. Stop pretending that anybody knows what an optimal organisational structure is until they've tried it. It is a patronising, even arrogant, fallacy that anyone can know what a better structure is in advance. It's the nature of complexity. We can only experiment in increments. Structure must be emergent, not imposed.

Similarly, culture is an emergent property of the complex work system. It is an output not an input. Change the attitudes and behaviours, then that becomes culture. Culture doesn't come in a tube to be inserted. What's more, we managers/consultants can't change culture. The community has to change itself, and want to do so. We can only change the conditions under our control and see what effect that has, then see what culture emerges. And that effect is unpredictable. Again, nobody knows. You have to suck it and see. Hence small steps.

For Example

Look at DevOps as an example. The point of DevOps is to span silos, not to change one set of silos into different ones. Changing from North/South slices into East/West slices is still slices. We see too many enterprises assuming one of the first steps of DevOps is a reorganisation. DevOps isn't about org structures. You can organise into functional technology silos with virtual product teams, or into product teams with virtual technology functions and guilds. Either way it is a matrix.

Most legacy enterprises are organised into functional teams. Although the current preference is for a product team instead and there is an argument that a team should stay together over the long term, the reality is that the size of the team will grow and shrink over time as the volume of change in the product varies. Therefore only a core will be constant anyway — the teams need to be fluid. So there is no downside to them being virtual teams taken from functional groups.

Moreover, the future is product teams brought together from multiple departments, not sourced exclusively from IT — someone from marketing, product design, digital design, shadow IT teams, third party suppliers, vendors. All the more reason for them to be virtual.

Your internal IT technical teams may want to regroup as providers of platforms, automation, tools, security etc, but there is no need to rush into that either until you understand exactly how it will work in your enterprise.

Get the DevOps working first, then a reorg may be an optimisation. When DevOps makes your people realise they need to restructure, then it is time. Pull not push.

Restructuring

It is enervating when the goal of the restructure is explicitly "to be more agile," but it is done in this one big bang. The irony. Finite step transformations (from "as-is" to "to-be") are big bets. Agile is supposed to be about making small bets with minimum blast radius. A restructure is never that. If you're truly agile, you will never (seldom?) do a big-bang restructure again.

Of all the dysfunctions of transformation, restructuring is one of the most damaging. We need to think again about the use of structural reorgs to chase "transformation." Don't do them.

» They don't work.

» They break existing teams.

» They damage morale.

» Reorgs just churn. They unsettle people and disrupt processes.

» They sow confusion.

» And they turn one set of silos into a different set of silos.

OK, sure they work sometimes. But, if a reorg is successful it's usually dumb luck and bloody toil. The consulting firms will *only* tell you about their successes: even a blind squirrel finds a few nuts. Some can be seen to have been done in a fairly successful and intentional way. It takes some very good and very strong people at many levels to pull it off.

But the exceptions just prove the rule, in fact I doubt there are exceptions that truly "succeed." It's likely just too narrow a definition of success. Reorgs are violent. They're done to people against their will and by force. They have all sorts of toxic cultural repercussions. This, at its heart, is my deepest objection to how reorganisation is done. What are the medium term consequences for psychological safety, for trust in management, and for real lasting change, when process reengineering and organisational restructure is designed behind closed doors then imposed by decree?

New Ways of Working

As everybody is surely aware by now, big things are afoot in how we think about work and management.

> » Agile has spilled out of IT into the enterprise.

> » Complex systems theory is finally shifting how we think.

> » Safety culture is revealing the value in failure.

> » Less widely known (yet): Open culture is flipping the hierarchy.

> » As well there are ideas like servant manager, transformational leader, open space, invitational leadership, promise theory, sustainability, and more...

They all aim for, as Jonathan Smart put it, "better value sooner, safer, happier." We simply call them the New Ways of Working and Managing.

This is a work renaissance. It is the biggest paradigm shift in management thinking in generations — certainly since the ideas of iterative improvement to flow, rooted in TWI (Training Within Industry) and blossoming in Lean; and maybe the biggest shift since Scientific Management a century ago.

Sound like an exaggeration? Let's look at the actual European Renaissance, paraphrased from Wikipedia (so it must be true):

Consider the Characteristics of the Renaissance

> » A focus on humanism: personkind as the driver of all thought, instead of abstract entities.

> » A resurfacing of learning from classical sources.

> » A flowering of literature, a greater sharing of ideas.

> » Depicting a more natural reality, model things on how they are not how we might stylise or imagine them.

» Reform learning for everybody, not just elites.

» Emphasise observation, data, and inductive reasoning.

» Upheaval, reform, disrupting the status quo.

The New Ways of Managing Do the Same

» Making work human again, treating people like people not resources, adults not children, and as if we are all on the same side.

» Building on work that goes back a century: scientific management (1900s), statistical production (1930s), Training Within Industry (1940s), Toyota Production System (1960s), Total Quality Management TQM (1980s), Lean (1990s), complex systems (2000s), Agile (2000s).

» A flow of management ideas flourishing on the Internet, coming from all directions: e-commerce, war, information technology, space travel, robotics, medicine, social policy, politics...

» Overcoming our cognitive biases and defeating the myth of simple systems; modelling how the world really works, not how we would like it to.

» Freeing knowledge workers to invent their own solutions instead of imposing models from gurus and consultancies.

» Making observation and experiment the centre of our work.

» Flipping the hierarchy, getting out of the way, bringing real work to the fore.

Communications and Networked Ways of Working Breaking Down Hierarchies

The Renaissance brought new ideas, a new culture, new ways of doing things, and a fresh start. The same is happening to management around the world, and has been for several decades — it's a management renaissance. This is important to you, to us all, for three reasons:

» It's time we got more humanity back into work. People aren't resources, they're colleagues.

» Repeatedly, we see organisations fail to advance ("transform") their work systems. These failures leave damage (including poisoning the terms "DevOps" and "Agile").

» The world urgently needs higher productivity to weather the coming economic storm.

We believe the key to unlock advancement to new ways of working is changing the ways we manage. That's why we wrote our book. We are trying to express and facilitate this renaissance.

Emergence

Organisational structure should emerge from the needs of the people, pulled by them not pushed on them. It should happen in an agile way — constantly reflecting, adjusting, and improving. Iterate, increment, experiment, explore. You can't make knowledge workers do anything. We have to stop *doing* change to people. If they don't want it, then that's the problem to be addressed. You can't force them to believe something different, or even to act in a different way. You can force slaves, manual workers, and clerical workers because you can see the output per person. Taylorism.

Knowledge workers work collaboratively on invisible work. You can't see it or measure it at the individual level. (Attempting to do so just ruins the benefits of teaming). All you can see is the team's results.

And they sure won't change in a matter of weeks or months. Humans aren't machines. We aren't Human Resources to be manipulated and engineered. There is a lot of deterministic thinking amongst consultants and thought leaders which we find distasteful.

Stop it. Be human.

About Rob England

Rob England is an independent management consultant, coach, trainer, and commentator based in Wellington, New Zealand. He usually works with his partner, Dr. Cherry Vu. Together as a team, they brand themselves as Teal Unicorn, transforming organisations to New Ways Of Working And Managing.

Rob is an internationally-recognised thought leader in DevOps and IT Service Management (ITSM) and a published author of seven books and many articles. He is best known for his recently retired controversial blog and alter-ego, the IT Skeptic. He speaks regularly at international conferences.

He has owned his own consulting company, Two Hills, since 2005. Before that, he had technical, management, and solutions roles for twenty years in the software industry.

Rob is a contributor to *The DevOps Handbook*, and to ITIL (2011 *Service Strategy* book, and minor contributions to two upcoming ITIL4 books), and a lead author of *VeriSM*. Rob was awarded the inaugural New Zealand IT Service Management Champion award for 2010 by itSMFnz, and made a Life Member in 2017.

About Dr. Cherry Vu

Vũ Anh Đào (Cherry Vu) is Chief Executive Officer of Two Hills, and a lead coach, trainer, and consultant in Vietnam.

Dr. Cherry Vu is an expert on training leaders; and an experienced consultant to government and business on organisational change, change management, and culture change. She has worked and studied in New Zealand, Germany, and Vietnam. She is the founder of the professional body Business Agility Vietnam.

She has helped business and public sector organisations develop their change management capabilities. Cherry applies the most practical skills and instruments to optimise their change outcomes with a goal of arming leaders, practitioners, and change agents. Lately she has been immersing herself in the IT industry, bringing a different perspective to help Rob with transformations.

Conclusion & Acknowledgments

Conclusion

"My, you sure love a good story, don't cha!"

—Mrs. Lovett, Sweeney Todd

The stories in this book are based upon real-word experience. Each author brings a unique perspective to either a massive failure, or how to set yourself up to have smaller failures than expected. The purpose of this type of information exchange is twofold.

First, we want you to know you are not alone. As the DevOps/DevSecOps communities continue to grow and share their experience, it gives us a chance to start to recognize patterns and develop processes for managing those patterns of failure. Second, we want you to participate in these exchanges, either by telling your personal journey in a presentation at All Day DevOps (alldaydevops.com), or by participating in your regional user groups, meeting your peers, and recognizing the patterns that might be unique in your specific area.

As a follow up to this book, we've already started planning the next edition. **The thought is to supplement the stories with a regular online monthly meeting to exchange stories with you and the Epic Failures authors.** Justin Miller has volunteered to help manage that initiative. Give him a call if you're interested in participating, or just want to talk about what you're working on. You can reach Justin at +1 (571) 336-2598, jmiller@sonatype.com.

If you enjoyed the book, we'd very much appreciate a 5-star review on Amazon. It will encourage others to join in our community, and continue to "fail." Failure is progress. May you have great "progress" in your upcoming ventures.

Mark Miller
Founder and Editor, DevSecOps Days Press
Co-Founder, All Day DevOps
Senior Storyteller, Sonatype

Acknowledgments

This book is the work of eleven authors, but a lot went on behind the scenes to make all the pieces work.

Thank you to the authors of Epic Failures, Volume 1 for being mentors and supporters of this edition: Aubrey Stearns, DJ Schleen, Caroline Wong, Fabian Lim, Chris Roberts, Chetan Conikee, Edwin Kwan, Stefan Streichsbier.

The support team who helped produce the book were indispensible for making sure the quality and presentation of the content was top notch: Alexis Del Duke and Nikki Mejer copy editors, Melissa Schmidt editing formatting and graphic design. A special shout out to the 100+ community members who volunteered their time to proofread the book and give invaluable feedback to the authors. Sincerely, thank you.

Finally, thank you to you, the reader, for contributing your valuable time to support the DevOps and DevSecOps Communities. We look forward to meeting you in person at upcoming DevSecOps Days (devsecopsdays.com), and online for All Day DevOps (alldaydevops.com).

SUPPORT FOR THE COMMUNITY

We couldn't have done this without the support of DevSecOps Days, All Day DevOps and Sonatype. They have provided funding, resources and moral support, making it possible to create a community environment that will continue to grow as the community matures.

We invite you to join us as a practitioner and as a contributor.

ABOUT DEVSECOPS DAYS PRESS

This is the second book in a series of "Epic Failures" from DevSecOps Days Press. We'll continue to provide stories from people and teams throughout the DevOps/ DevSecOps Communities in future editions. Join us at DevSecOpsDays.com to see the most recent listing of events around the world, hear the DevSecOps Podcast Series, and have access to free downloads of both "Epic Failures" books.

You're welcome to reach out to the authors for further discussion by following them on Linkedin, Twitter and various community forums.

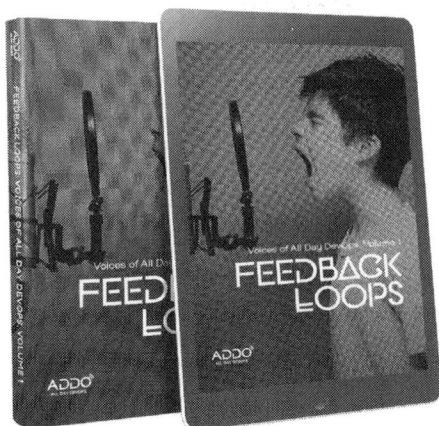

Made in the USA
Coppell, TX
05 February 2020